PRIVACY CRISIS BANKING

BANK SECRECY PLAN & RESOURCE GUIDE
to Protect
IDENTITY, MONEY, and PROPERTY

GRANT HALL

Published by James Clark King, LLC, Las Vegas, Nevada

For information on our products, please make inquiries through our website at www.PrivacyCrisis.com.

Certain names and company names cited in the text for illustration purposes are fictitious names and are not meant to describe real people or businesses.

Note: References in this book sourced to the Internet were current as of the date of publication.

Figures in this book:

LCCN: 2011934821

11 12 13 14 15 • 5 4 3 2 1

ISBN 10: 0-9786573-3-0
ISBN 13: 978-0-9786573-3-8

Contents

Dedication

To Victoria.

Acknowledgment

The author wishes to acknowledge the team that helped produce
Privacy Crisis Banking.

Disclaimer

This book is sold as a privacy book and resource guide. The author and publisher are not offering professional advice pertaining to the law, in any jurisdiction. Accounting, tax, or other professional advice is not provided in this book. Readers should consult professionals for their questions about these and other matters and are encouraged to follow the laws in their given jurisdiction and to never break the law in efforts to obtain personal or business privacy.

Efforts have been made to make the information and resources contained in this book as accurate as possible. Obtaining personal and business privacy has been accomplished by many through the information provided herein. However, resource information and policies of businesses and government agencies change from time to time, and these policies and trends may be different in various locations throughout the world. Thus, neither the author nor publisher can guarantee the application of privacy principles or resources as written in this book.

While all information was believed to be correct at the time of publication, both content and typographical errors may be present. The book should be used as a guide, and its content accuracy could have changed following the date it was printed.

Privacy Crisis Banking is an educational and entertainment book. The author and publisher will not be liable or responsible for any personal or entity losses caused or believed to be caused by information contained in the book.

Those who do not want to accept full responsibility for themselves and their businesses and agree to the above disclaimer may return the book to the publisher for a refund.

Introduction

Writing an information book is a tremendous responsibility. Holding yourself out as an expert and making promises to deliver, on paper, requires stamina for proper research, time to prepare the most up-to-date information, and confidence to selectively recommend the most practical and cost-effective methods, tactics, and principles that will empower readers to succeed.

Privacy Crisis Banking evolved over a period of three years following readers' requests for more information and resources on bank secrecy and financial privacy after publication of my first book, *Privacy Crisis*. Demand for business and personal privacy resources and tactics has soared during the last few years—a time period during which certain traditional banking havens have lost their prestige and reputations as a safe place to store money, and as a result, investors' and savers' confidence has waned, due to piercings of some of these countries' bank secrecy laws by U.S. government agencies and private entities alike.

Governments and companies under contract with government agencies, sue-happy lawyers, disgruntled exes, identity thieves, and other criminals are on a money- and property-seizure binge. Both companies' and individuals' assets are at risk of being confiscated, and these wealth transfers or thefts are increasing at alarming rates, as gross tax receipts fail to cover government agencies' overhead expenses and inflated workers' salaries. Meanwhile, white collar criminals—those working within the system and those on the outside—connive to steal from those who have accumulated wealth or have the ability to pay judgments or penalties over the long term.

While public awareness increases on the subject of money and property privacy, certain media sources continue to act as mouthpieces for the administration, proclaiming that privacy is dead in the water. They maintain that the government and selected companies have a right to citizens' personal and confidential financial records, real property details, and other fascist-like propaganda nonsense. All this is designed to foster dependence and to brainwash the masses of the uninformed, sway the non-committed consumer, and persuade all others to accept the con job as it is fed to them by certain hosts of television and radio shows. These commentators continue reading from their masters' script with Orwellian, hypnotic persuasion, while claiming to be on their audiences' side.

My organization of the selected material contained in this book will provide specific how-to information on bank secrecy and financial privacy today, in real time, and in the aftermath of the most privacy-invasive period in the history of the United States of America. Real case histories are cited when applicable to the subject heading, though the names, in most cases, have been changed to protect identity and privacy. Additionally, financial institutions and other business resources are included that will enable the astute individual and business manager to obtain money and property privacy at the highest level possible.

To bank in secrecy and have privacy in all of your financial affairs is possible. These are the same principles, concepts, methods, and resources many use to insulate themselves from confiscation attacks. I promise you that this information will work for you, as it has for me.

Grant Hall
Western U.S.A
November, 2011

♦ ONE ♦

Ivory Tower Pirates

"We're putting up with the federal government on so many fronts, and nearly every month they come out with another hare-brained scheme...to tell us that our life is going to be better if we just buckle on some other kind of rule or regulation. And we usually just play along for a while. We ignore 'em for as long as we can. We try not to bring it to a head but if it comes to a head we found that it's best to tell them to go to Hell and run the state the way you want to run your state."

—Brian Schweitzer, Governor of Montana

BARTER COMPANY SEIZED BY GOVERNMENT

The money, precious metals, and equipment of the barter company Liberty Services were seized by F.B.I. agents on November 14, 2007, with a financial "shock and awe"–like surprise attack. Confiscated were more than 200,000 troy ounces of silver coins, silver bars, and silver scrap, thousands of pounds of copper coins, over 200 troy ounces of gold coins, platinum coins, and dies, molds, and casts. In addition, a company bank account valued at over a quarter of a million dollars was taken over by the government.

The company offered a means of exchange for goods and services. Bartering is legal, in lieu of using money. People may use other agreed-upon exchanges besides United States dollars for transactions, according to Federal Reserve spokesman, Andrew Williams, who stated:

> "There is no law that says goods and services must be paid for with Federal Reserve notes. Parties entering into a transaction can establish any medium of exchange that is agreed upon."[1]

In addition to company assets being seized, customers' property—bought and paid for medallions—was also taken during the raid by the federal government. The Liberty Dollar was the barter company's asset-backed barter tool, used for the trading of goods and services and accepted by thousands of merchants and individual users throughout the country. They served as receipts with intrinsic value. According to an article written by syndicated investigative reporter Michael Webster in *Bonds Market*, S & A Digest has described these as follows:

"It's essentially a warehouse receipt you can use to barter for goods. Each Liberty Dollar is a receipt for so much gold, silver, and copper."[2]

WITHOUT DUE PROCESS?

Was this a war-like asset seizure of a private company by government's hired guns, a heist approved through the authorization of a judge, an "administrative order" *only*? Whether due process was used to close down the company is questionable. One article suggests that the F.B.I. and the Department of Justice did not use the injunction process to close down NORFED, nor did a federal judge issue an order for the company to discontinue business.[3] Was the business, Liberty Services, previously NORFED (The National Organization for the Repeal of the Federal Reserve and Internal Revenue Codes), such a threat after a decade of operation that it warranted an F.B.I. seizure without an injunction or trial? And was this seizure a "Soviet-Style Attack on NORFED?"[4] Lending support to this being a communist-style takeover is a quote of the CEO of the company that produced the Liberty Dollars, Dan Priest, who said, "There's been no legal cease-and-desist order."[5] Is it true that "all federal agents had was a search warrant issued by a magistrate?"[6] One article states that a cease and desist order was provided to NORFED during 2006.[7] Verification on whether the company was "legally ordered" to stop business may be questioned, but Liberty Services founder Bernard von NotHaus claims that "they had never started any legal action."[8] It has been claimed that the goal of the government was to put the company out of business, due to the awareness of many about the devaluation of the U.S. dollar and the gaining credibility of the privately issued barter currency, strictly a voluntary means of exchange by those businesses and individuals choosing to use it.

Whatever the "process" used to close the ten-year-old barter company, U.S. Magistrate Judge Dennis L. Howell signed the seizure warrant on November 9, 2007, as F.B.I. Special Agent Andrew F. Romagnuolo signed an Application and Affidavit for Seizure Warrant, sealing the company's fate, while claiming the holdings were forfeitable to the United States, due to money laundering, mail fraud, and wire fraud.[9]

WHIPPING CAPITAL HORSES

Have fascist-style "administrative orders," by judges, supported by agency heads, made the risk-reward ratio for successful, first-world style entrepreneurship unrealistic—a fantasy—due to the "trigger happy," banana republic–like, expedited rulings by force of the U.S. government, without proper and lawful due process?

How can the prudent would-be management of a start-up or purchased business be expected to assume the hidden risks of government's "weapons of mass destruction" dismantling of their proprietary business creations, labor, and investors' capital? And all this, accomplished by agency men gone mad, who recruit co-conspirators—"lawbreakers who preside in black robes"—whose signatures, along with the force of hired guns, cause business plan terminations and facilitate the seizure of equipment, property, money, and accounts, transferring these once–privately owned properties into government coffers.

The most sound business plans—backed by in-depth empirical product and service testing, supported by statistically measured, high-probability-for success confidence levels, and promising marketing success with proven customer acceptability—cannot succeed, when basic freedom losses occur within the business's registered jurisdiction and when force overrides morality and equal justice for all.

Has freedom of the once-free people in the United States of America been destroyed by guises, trickery, "laws of persuasion" (unread, but passed), "redlining," and redirection by bought-off controllers, who are now the powerhouses of government agencies declaring war on "subjects" who exercise freedom practices through free market buying and selling?

When ongoing businesses' and individuals' capital and creations hang by a single thread, awaiting being sniped by "scissor-happy," politically motivated administrators—judges, agency officers, and officials—and when the power-hungry, budget-poor, bloated, and bankrupt Big Bureaucrat "suits" direct their "hired gangsters" to "steal," declare war on free market risk-takers, and take property without following the legal protocol of giving both sides their day in court—then, the residents and businessmen and businesswomen *should* fear for their livelihood and economic survival and maybe their lives, too. Are we experiencing fascism in America today? Yes.

DEFENSIVE MEASURES TO FASCIST SEIZURES

As protective defenses against money and property seizures, prudent business managers and individuals now "require" "self-insurance" plans and non-traditional money and property secrecy methods, in order to survive and guard against the potential threats of a debt-ridden, famished, bankrupt, and sometimes violent government out of control. And how should the sometimes-masked pirates—the "authorized" agents of force employed by the fascist dictatorship—be dealt with, when they confront and steal from private business managers' companies' and individuals alike, without following the rule of law? Can the case be made for dealing with such irrational, apparently "brain-dead" and brain-washed order-takers on an individual case basis through the court system—trying them individually and separately from their employing agencies, while not allowing for their immunity from prosecution—civil or criminal—as has been traditionally offered to police and agency enforcers by the courts?

THE END OF "LIBERTY"

Liberty Dollar was founded as NORFED Corporation by Bernard von NotHaus in 1998 and was created as a "private, voluntary barter currency."[10] The company provided a means of trading for goods and services and was promoted as a private **voluntary** barter currency, advertising itself as same.

"According to the Liberty Dollar's web site the Liberty Dollar was a private voluntary barter currency (PVBC)."[11]

The actual website of the company has reportedly been removed by court order.

Long before the company became popular through their multilevel marketing system and growing awareness of the privately-owned Federal Reserve, in 1999, nearly a decade prior to the company's fall, the U.S. Treasury performed an investigation on NORFED, determining that silver reserves were adequate to exchange for their certificates and finding that their receipts did not meet the definition of counterfeit money.[12] But government agents took a second look at the company, once the medallions were minted, and claims were made that the company advertised these as "real money," and it was believed by some that certain merchants might mistake the privately issued barter medallions as legal tender money.

Liberty Dollar founder Bernard von NotHaus and three others, including Sarah Jane Bledsoe, Rachelle J. Moseley, and William Kevin Innes, were arrested in June, 2009 and have been indicted on a number of charges involving conspiracy and fraud.[13]

ALTERNATIVE CURRENCIES BOOMING

Aware citizens are unhappy with the U.S. dollar's serious devaluation, estimated by some to be a 97 percent loss in buying power since the Federal Reserve Act of 1913. Conversely, gold and silver have historically retained their purchasing power throughout recorded history. Commodity, asset-backed currencies make perfect economic sense, though gold and silver do not necessarily have to be the chosen store of value to make the money sound. But printing excessive dollars for immediate credit, without collateral backing these receipts—as does the U.S. central bank—is a sure road to currency value disaster. People and groups are becoming more aware of this fraud.

New alternative currencies being used by communities are gaining momentum, even after the demise of Liberty Services' Liberty Dollar.

Berkshares, Inc., a Massachusetts-based company, has a wide and growing acceptability of its alternative, voluntary "Berkshares" for the benefit of local businesses accepting the tool for exchange.

"BerkShares are a local currency designed for use in the Berkshire region of Massachusetts issued by BerkShares, Inc., a non-profit organization working in collaboration with participating local banks, businesses, and non-profit organizations."[14]

A North Carolina community is printing its own currency. "The Plenty" is used primarily in the Chatham county town of Pittsboro.[15]

"Detroit Cheers" is a barter, voluntary currency, spendable at some local businesses.

"Detroit Cheers is a new local currency—the city version of exchanging grain for flour or darned socks for a loaf of bread."[16]

The script concept was commonly used during the Great Depression. Local currencies may very well be the answer, in part, to the monopoly greed machine that has ruined consumers' purchasing power and mortgaged future generations.

DEBT MACHINE CONQUERER?

Perhaps the very nature of the business of the claimed barter company,

NORFED, was the entire reason for it becoming a target that needed to be "rubbed out." Did the money creators from the debt machine—the private-corporation central bank of the United States of America, the Federal Reserve System, and their contract partner, the United States Treasury—believe that NORFED, a precious metals, asset-backed system of exchange on an ascending growth curve and a contributor to public awareness on the meaning of "money," posed a potential "problem" for the U.S. central bank's continued credibility? Yes, according to some supporters.

"The dollar is going down the tubes, and this is something that can protect the value of their money, and the Federal Reserve is threatened by that. It'll definitely fire people up."[17] And did NORFED's growth and increased popularity and readily available receipts, digital credits, and medallions—being accepted by increasing numbers of businesses for bartering goods and services—threaten to take market share from the Federal Reserve System's monopoly-like member commercial banks? Undoubtedly, without question, yes.

How will the Federal Reserve and government agencies handle the new crop of those aforementioned alternative currencies and many more that are springing up? Can they close them all through trumped-up legal charges, based on flimsy interpretations and biased judgment calls justified on technicalities? Perhaps for a while. Or will these local currencies escape the wrath of Big Bureaucrat due to their carefully claimed status of local, alternative barter currencies? Or will the sheer numbers of these currencies be too overwhelming for funded government goons to overturn?

As awareness grows, the many "followers" of the Liberty Dollar model are not only gaining ground with their numbers but are gaining support from communities, even banks, making it less likely they will go down easily if they are attacked.

A close look at the recent bosses who have manned the store that prints the Fed's "funny money"—the "monopoly" currency system currently in force and its use being enforced—may provide some clues on the future trends of banking and money in the U.S.A.

"MONEYCHANGER" BOSSES

Alan Greenspan, former Federal Reserve Board chairman for a period of about two decades, once supported an asset-backed currency system. His apparent full-circle flip-flop, from believing in money backed by tangible assets to becoming the Fed boss, is noteworthy, as the U.S. dollar is a currency from debt creation *only*—a currency with "perception of value" and not tangible market worth.

The Federal Reserve System is the epitome of irresponsible "fiat money," without tangibles contributing to its value, and the "business plan" of the Fed is surely an unsound one, were *success* of the money system the goal of the central bank. It is not.

The certain course is toward a loss of purchasing power for the population, who must use such a perpetually devaluing money for the purchase of their goods and services and for investment capital. This money, created from debt and leveraged (low member bank reserve requirements), is not intended to be repaid entirely, as you would repay a loan, but its objective is a limitless credit expansion plan for the immediate financial gratification and profit of those being issued the instant credit.

Greenspan's early publication (1966) supported a money system with assets (gold) backing the receipts (money). Indeed, the long-time FRB-appointed boss appears to have been for sale to the highest bidder, based on his 180-degree turnaround, from supporting asset-backed currency (gold), to currency created without collateral, except through "indentured slavery" forces applied to the "helpless" citizenry, by causing losses of purchasing power and mandatory taxation without representation.

Greenspan wrote *Gold and Economic Freedom*. "Under a gold standard, the amount of credit an economy can support is determined by the economy's tangible assets, since every credit instrument is ultimately a claim on some tangible asset,"[18] he wrote. One wonders how such a political and economic belief system shift could have occurred— at least it appears to have occurred—as the Fed has no tangible asset-backed system, and Greenspan captained that greed-based sinking ship for some two decades or so. And even though it had been years from the publication of *Gold and Economic Freedom* until his appointment as Federal Reserve Board chairman by President Ford, Greenspan apparently reversed his thinking, from advocating sound, asset-backed currency, to non-asset backed currency—money created from debt for "loans" to the United States of America from "thin air assets." Why, this man, based on his published work and his early career, "claimed devotion" to responsible, asset-backed, money-as-receipts for tangible assets (gold), as evidenced by *Gold and Economic Freedom*, would have made a fine "chairman" for NORFED Corporation, the now-defunct asset-backed barter company put out of business by the same government that is under contract with Greenspan's former company (Federal Reserve Act of 1913)—the Federal Reserve System. Instead of practicing his documented early economic "beliefs" pertaining to money, Mr. Greenspan spent a great portion of his career as a pseudo-politician, arguably "the world's most powerful man," while at the helm of the greatest and most irresponsible, non-asset–backed, money-from-debt monetary system in the history of the world—the central bank of the United States of America, the privately owned Federal Reserve.

Current Federal Reserve Chairman Ben Bernanke looks the part of a bank officer—until he opens his mouth. As the "80-something" chairman, Alan Greenspan—the long-winded Ph.D. intellectual with academic speech, put-you-to-sleep "tone," and carefully selected "academic" words to match his "Doctor" credentials—exited the scene, little-known Ben Shalom Bernanke, former Princeton economics department head, was appointed the leader of the most powerful central bank in the world. In spite of his academic research at Harvard and MIT, where he devoted his studies to the monetary causes of the great depression,[19] Mr. Bernanke, speaking in a rather medium-high–pitched voice, "verbally trembling" and sounding feminine in tone on occasion but with clear diction as he is drilled by representatives, is without a doubt ruining what is left of the purchasing power of the U.S. dollar. And although appearing nervous, even fearful, by way of his subtle verbal clues, the balding, gray-bearded Bernanke exhibits arrogance not previously seen by Fed bosses. Aware viewers recognize his inadequacy, as do highly respected investors and businessmen. According to Jim Rogers, chairman of Rogers Holdings and one of the most successful investors in the world, Bernanke is hardly up to the task, knows little about the field of economics and currency, and "all he knows about is printing money and making mistake after mistake."[20]

He sets monetary policy—the excess creation of dollars for cronies' "bailouts," that have created a "second great depression," perhaps by design—again, eight decades hence following number one. Not only has the Fed printed and entered computerized digital dollar credits, rather than allow free market systems to work, this excessive money from debt is not only unsound, it is clearly politically motivated, and these "bailouts," are, without a doubt, for favors to the "too big to fail" groups. Bernanke has refused to reveal where 2.2 trillion dollars were allocated to fund at least part of the 2008 "bailout," and when questioned by Vermont Senator Sanders[21] about which institutions received this money—entries that substantially dilute the dollar's purchasing power and will become the taxpayers' "permanent" obligation, this "debt from debt," a recognized scam by the public and not wanted by the citizenry, as measured by reliable polls—the Fed boss refused a truthful answer, saying "no," he would not provide the names of the institutions receiving the money. Further, this Ivy League professor "genius" again refused ("I don't know") to provide Congressman Alan Grayson with the names of foreign banks that received half a trillion dollars of money "printed" from debt by the Fed to hand out to foreigners without accountability.[22]

Devaluation of the U.S. Dollar, 1914-2010

Dark area represents 4% of retained purchasing power, light area is 96%, the amount of value consumers have lost for buying goods and services since the Federal Reserve Act, December, 1913.

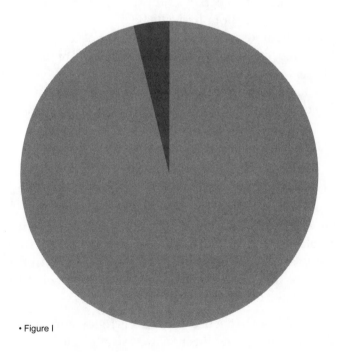

• Figure I

"Since the creation of the Federal Reserve in 1913, the dollar has lost 96% of its purchasing power. In other words, $100 today buys only 4% of the amount of goods or services that it would have in 1913."[23]

"RULERS"

The objective individual who is capable of critical thinking and checking footnotes has to draw only one conclusion: Americans have lost their freedom and are being ruled by force, by corporations that rule government, mainly, the controllers of the Federal Reserve System. And this central bank did not even originate in the United States of America.

> "The blunt reality is that the Rothschild banking dynasty in Europe was the dominate force, both financially and politically, in the formation of the Bank of the United States."[24]

How do these criminals, a.k.a. the "Fed," and their enforcers, affect your freedom and money and property privacy rights? Greatly. Assets will, without cause, be seized and taken over to support the debt machine. Unless, that is, measures are taken to safeguard them, while using non-traditional bank secrecy and property protection that legally cannot be pierced or cannot physically be discovered.

While the Federal Reserve "figureheads" do not represent the source of the deep-seated, multi-generational "family affair" of the true controllers, they do serve as recognizable "proclaimed rulers" over freedom and free men. Just ask them. According to Alan Greenspan, the Federal Reserve is not accountable to the government, as per his response to a question by newsman Jim Lehrer. "Lehrer asked Greenspan what should be the proper relationship between the Chairman of the Fed and the President of the United States."[25] Greenspan's shocking reply was:

> "Well, first of all, the Federal Reserve is an independent agency, and that means basically, that there is no other agency of the government which can overrule actions that we take. So long as that this is in place and there is no evidence that the administration or the congress or anybody else is requesting that we do things other than what we think is the appropriate thing, then what the relationships are don't frankly matter."[26]

Based on what has happened to your currency-devaluation and reduction of purchasing power through excessive "printed" dollars and the "unauthorized bailouts" of 2008 adding more fuel to the currency fire, and the blatant fascist remarks of the contracted Federal Reserve's former chief, your country has, without question, been taken over by a corporation at least partially controlled by foreign stockholders, and this corporation now rules ("corporatism") by force and is accountable to no one, not even your elected President of the United States of America.

CONDITIONS AND MANIPULATIONS

As expansion of credit provides for capital goods purchases for businesses and for high-dollar consumer goods, manufacturing equipment, machinery, second homes, boats, recreational vehicles, and more are purchased, as credit is eased. Booms occur, and bubbles form, break, shatter, or run out of air, leading to the inevitable contraction phase of the economic cycle—a time period that, in total, may span years but that is highly dependent on "underlying conditions." And the Fed's money policy influences the cycles' "character," of course, as money from thin air fuels the cycle, and easy credit allows for aggressive businesses to attempt to gain greater success with a "friendly Fed." Investors, too, may have opportunities, until unscheduled events occur. The piper has to be paid. But paid only with a greater fiat money supply and with greater fools to pay higher portions of their earnings to support banks and political favorites being "bailed out"—and through losses of purchasing power, higher taxes, taxes on income, and all other tariffs, hidden and obvious, which "rulers" control.

The squeezing of the middle class, the salaried class, causes the living standard and balance sheets of most to suffer, and they, like strangled, struggling, suffocating, assaulted victims, "gasp for breath and energy" to support first-world lifestyles, as do overly regulated businesses—especially those debt-ridden businesses—and the captured can't break free from the mighty hands of the criminal octopus to escape, and instead, perish. Except for a few, that is.

Strong minds with the motivation to learn and succeed, at any age, are the assets necessary to legally conquer the conquerors. The "enemies" are too busy, their hired hands are too slow, and they have less drive and desire less, than the dedicated freedom thinker. Your privacy rights can be obtained for all aspects of your life. Claiming independence, gaining knowledge, and a careful study of proven freedom principles and concepts and necessary privacy resources, will be your keys to succeed to whatever degree you so choose.

STATES SEIZE CITIZENS PROPERTY TO BALANCE BUDGETS

Of all the blatant, unconscionable abuses of power ever recorded, the seizing of the assets of the dead or claimed dead by government, and their failing to return money and property following truthful discovery, has to rank as some of the most immoral, outright disgusting behavior on record by government.

Class action lawsuits? Sure and punitive damages, as allowed by statute. How about prison sentences for the thieves in charge of returning the property, who never did their duty but kept residents' "stored labor" (money), heirlooms, intangible property, and keepsakes?

Claiming to seize and hold unclaimed property that isn't really unclaimed is a practice states have been involved in, with the seized property being used to balance states' budgets.[27] Banks are required to turn over unclaimed property to states when deaths occur to account holders. "The problem is that states return less than a quarter of unclaimed property to the rightful owners."[28]

Based on a "Good Morning America" story, the practice is not an isolated incident, as states engage in the unlawful, profitable practice to fund their governments. Seizures of "unclaimed property" have been used to balance state budgets.[29] And the value of the unreturned property is substantial. How about $32 billion worth of unclaimed property?

> "The 50 U.S. states are holding more than $32 billion worth of unclaimed property that they're supposed to safeguard for their citizens. But a 'Good Morning America' investigation found some states aggressively seize property that isn't really unclaimed and then use the money—your money—to balance their budgets."[30]

Bank of America claimed that safety deposit holder Carla Ruff's safety deposit box owner was unknown, when in fact, her name and home address—a location just six blocks away from the Noe Valley Bank of America location—was inside the very box that was seized and turned over to the state of California. Not only was Ms. Ruff's box opened and her privacy invaded, but important paperwork inside the paid-up box was destroyed—shredded—and these documents were needed, as her husband was dying at the time. Jewelry owned by Ms. Ruff worth an estimated $82,000, as per an appraisal, had been auctioned off. Ruff and other Californians have filed a class-action lawsuit against the state of California[31]

BANKS AND BROKERS "STEAL" CUSTOMERS' MONEY

There's an epidemic "financial disease" going around in America today that sickens the customers of certain brokerage firms and banks. Some of these institutions have balance sheets propped up by illiquid, near-worthless, derivative-like issues, or just plain old debt that can't be paid or isn't likely to be paid. And to compensate and keep these firms afloat, employees of these "bucket shops" and insolvent companies—bankrupt firms, if mark to market practices were used, and "banks" in name only—practice third-world tactics or worse, hoodwinking customers and hiding behind numerical employee codes, telephone voice mail, and delayed e-mail responses, all the while keeping customers' accounts "frozen"and thus unavailable for cash withdrawals, transfer, or closure. These delays, holds, pretext games, or outright thefts are clearly designed to keep customers' money under institutions' control.

Is this type of blatant customer account abuse white collar criminal theft? IF money is taken from one entity by another without authorization, expedited civil penalties, at the very least, should be used to put a stop to it, and perhaps criminal theft charges should be strongly considered as well. And why should individuals working for these institutions, who were smart enough to be hired and given the responsibility to "manage" customer accounts, be let off the hook and permitted to hide behind the corporate shield of the business paying them, to continue abusing their fiduciary responsibility, in some cases, and be immune from civil lawsuit damages, individually, or be free from being charged with crimes as individuals? They should not. And if fair and legitimate practices with reasonable agency oversight were implemented, instead of the "dog and pony show" Securities and Exchange Commission that has long been in place, along with banking regulatory agencies that are equally as irresponsible, customers would not suffer the hardships that are fully documented herein. This merger of corporations' interests with government's "regulatory agencies" strongly resembles what Mussolini considered "corporatism," and is commonly known as fascism.

Portions of actual customers' bank and brokerage account horror stories' are quoted below:

> "We transferred $35,000 into Etrade several months ago. They have put a hold on our account for no apparent reason. We cannot transfer any money or pay bills. They cannot explain why there is a hold on our account. This is crazy!"[32]

> "Hi last week etrade flagged my account with more that 55K. They deactivated my account i cant log in or see any of my stocks, they would not tell me the reason, all they say if i have anything to ask, ill have to do it in writing. Please tell me what should i do?"[33]

"Dishonest SOB's. [Editor's note: This post refers to E-Trade and is one of the posted complaints at www.rateitall.com.] They froze my account with more than a 100K total assets. After a mix up with another account, I received a terse letter explaining while they are sorry, they took all appropriate actions! The only problem is, I was told the matter would be cleared up in just 24 hours. . . when it initially occurred. 7 and half months later, SEVEN AND A HALF MONTHS later they send me a non-apology, in essence. I am begun legal proceedings against them. Absolutely the worst!"[34]

It may be that pretentious behavior and outright lies to the customer are motivated by greed. In fact, extra use of a customer's money and fees generated from the account—without servicing it or allowing the customer to use it—have been fully documented, and financial institutions have manipulated personnel and used time advantages to thwart customers' efforts to resolve account problems.[35]

"At eight months after the fraud discovery was confirmed—eight months of trying to communicate with officials and a fraud department who were oddly unavailable or unresponsive—I received a form letter from the WaMu Fraud Department advising me that according to the regulations, I had had a six month window for taking action; and (since WaMu had played out the clock for eight months) the letter asserted that I had waited 'too long' and my case was closed."[36]

Customers' bank accounts are vulnerable to "inside jobs," and losses have occurred when bank employees and contractors working for banks commit bank robbery right under the bank's nose. One Wells Fargo bank employee has been charged with stealing $100,000 as she wired funds from customer accounts into an account under her control.[37]

"Wells Fargo was able to retract some of the money, so the actual loss was $41,000, prosecutors said."[38]

One insider stole from other insiders and made off with over a million dollars following the theft of personal information stolen from 2,000 bank employees.[39]

"Adeniyi Adeyemi, 27, used his position as a contract computer technician at the bank's headquarters to steal the personal identifying information of 2,000 employees, most of whom worked in the IT department. Over an eight-year span, he used the information to set up dummy bank accounts in the employees' names and then transfer stolen funds from at least 11 charities throughout the world."[40]

While customer security is closely scrutinized by "customer service" when account holders attempt to access their accounts with financial institutions, in some cases, and certain customers' money, with E-Trade, for example, are inaccessible to these customers for months and months (see previously quoted complaints against E-Trade in this chapter), entry-level employees and certain "managers" do not seem to be subjected to the same level of oversight by those in upper management, lest fewer bank customer dissatisfaction cases and complaints would be reported by customers, and fewer "bank jobs" by insiders would happen. What recourse does a customer have, when his or her money is stolen—either through an obvious theft or by cover ups—negligence designed to keep the bank from covering losses incurred but to leave the customer with a drained account? If losses are not voluntarily covered by the financial institution that erred, the customer must initiate legal action against the company entrusted to secure the account, and this can be a costly, time-consuming ordeal, but may be the only recourse when losses are substantial. Author Naomi Wolf's lawsuit against J. P. Morgan Chase & Company, the legal successor to Washington Mutual Bank ("WaMu"), was filed on August 17, 2010, as a result of actual losses from her account exceeding $330,000, and according to Ms. Wolf's filing, "Defendant repeatedly ignored its legal responsibility to protect its clients' accounts, including ignoring and misleading Ms. Wolf's counsel on several occasions."[41]

BANKER ACCUSED OF STEALING A MILLION

Wondering who to trust at the financial services company where your money is kept can be a risky riddle. And sometimes the funds aren't just frozen for long periods of time to keep the institution in control of the money, but rather, are stolen outright by officials in charge of the account. A trust officer is accused of stealing one million dollars from an elderly widow's trust fund account. Gregory Phillip Burns, a trust officer at Colorado Business Bank, has been charged with eight counts of felony theft relating to losses from a trust fund account set up by a lady's late husband for the benefit and welfare of the elderly woman.[42] "A bank review found several withdrawals, each between $20,000 and $30,000 had been made from the trust to pay bills for Burns' credit card, according to court records."[43]

Based on the documented happenings related in this chapter and elsewhere in this book, clearly, individuals and businesses alike are at risk of having property and money "frozen," stolen, or seized by financial institutions and government agencies, and others.

RHODES' GRACE

When I was a boy in grade school, a community bank president trekked through the brush, timber, and prairie each fall with my Father and me, sometimes over a two- or three-successive-day period. The harvested fields' leftover grains, beautiful autumn colors of fallen oak and elm leaves, brown grass, and the natural habitat provided feed and cover for game birds sought by "working dogs," and the "hunts" were purposeful—as much for an informal inspection of our farm ranch by Country National Bank president Ross Andrews Rhodes, as for the "harvesting" of quail. The banker, a man in his 60s at the time, was a seasoned bank officer who had assumed the post of "troubleshooter" for banks in several states, over what was known to be a distinguished career. A shrewd Southerner, graduated from "ole Miss" ("worked my way through"), he was tall, with a ruddy complexion, likable, balding, and well-mannered. He spoke with a New Orleans–deep South mixture drawl, was sophisticated, yet tolerant and patient of those who weren't, and claimed to have once been the owner of "nineteen bird dogs." Today, he had only one, a Pointer—spotted, bred to find birds with his keen nose, showing his Master their spot for "flushing" them out, and having the patience to "hold a point" *forever*, if need be.

Mr. Rhodes had replaced "Doss," fired by the board and rumored to have committed two terminable offenses: signing on the dotted line for a "bankrupt" brother-in-law and running around on his *Missus*. And the previous president seldom made trips himself to local farms or ranches, delegating "inspections" to McNabb or Dewey, capable vice presidents who called me by name during check endorsements and deposit transactions. On occasion, each stamped my passbook, events that raised eyebrows of locals waiting to be attended to by bankers themselves—an attention grabber, this "special treatment" for a skinny, shy, "country boy" having not yet reached puberty. Rhodes, however, unlike his predecessor, was out of the bank often, preferring to meet customers face-to-face, not delegate to vp's "just getting a line on things" or looking for reasons to hunt during business hours, "killing two birds with one stone." *He was President.* And he knew it.

Days of the annual meet-up began with a morning chat by the fire, Rhodes' thermos replenishment with Mother's freshly made brew, which he took black, and his request for a second cinnamon roll prior to heading out. About noon, "limits" were reached, the dogs were half worn-out, and we hunters returned to the house, prepared for "dinner," and gathered around the table. Mr. Rhodes said grace. He began in a somewhat loud voice, though still at a decibel level comfortable to the ears—a high, though masculine "holler-like" pitch, head raised, eyes closed. Peeking, I noticed him, calling on "high" to be heard, asking for "blessings" for the food, his gracious hosts, Mom and Dad, their children—all mentioned by name—"good crop prices," the livestocks' health, the state of the country, guidance for "wars and rumors of wars,"—all were covered, along with *"help"* with the weather, business conditions, and relatives' health, ours and his own. The ordeal of his saying grace lasted several minutes, and what had started with bountiful verbal energy aplenty, after a time became the noticeable winding down phase of the prayer, as he neared its completion, and few new breaths had interrupted his "sermon," it being a shorter version, but not all that dissimilar to some of the less-abbreviated ones "Brother Waggons," had practiced in the same room, but without the sweat. And the long-anticipated "Amen" was welcomed by hungry, fidgeting kids. Wild game shot the day before was the "main dish" for "dinner," along with vegetables "canned" using a pressure cooker, opened from sealed lids on glass jars, potatoes and wild game gravy, everything "raised" on the soil we had just trampled over, "homemade light bread," Mr. Rhodes' favorite, pecan pie—and he had second helpings of each.

Later, the tour of the livestock began. Sheep and hogs in their pens were viewed, along with 4-H projects, stock not mortgaged but of interest to the president, "Grant's pens," the "show stock," and later, a pick-up truck trip to the pastures to see cows and their late-spring born calves nearly ready to be weaned. King Ranch "Peppy San" descendant, "Buck"—a chestnut sorrel purchased as a colt and a cutting horse with "cow" from birth, then being ridden by Dad and I *only*, he was not a kid's pony—was allowed to show his talent as my mount on certain of these occasions, as a prize heifer or herd bull was cut from the herd to show our efforts in quality beef cattle production. The confirming of bits and pieces, dotting of "i's" and crossing of "t's" was accomplished as the day wound down, in the barn, as Buck was unsaddled, brushed, and fed, or while riding inside the truck, amidst the Ford's straining engine's struggle to climb rocky hills or make it through ungraded, gravel-free, muddy roads. I, too, was questioned and discussed the balancing of livestock's rations, referencing *Morton's Feeds and Feeding Abridged,* with Country National Bank president Ross Andrews Rhodes listening and looking on.

Mother's home-cooked meals no doubt enticed Mr. Rhodes into being our repeat guest each year, and while not realizing her business contribution, my mother's healthy and hearty food and warm hospitality seemingly made "loan approvals" sail through without delay, or in the absence of paperwork, be finalized with, "Sure, we can do that," or "Just sign the note next time you're down at the bank," or sealed with a handshake, as much for respectful acknowledgment as for an agreement to pay the new debt.

One memorable post-wild game meal encounter with the bank's president is deeply embedded in my psyche. The late fall wind whistled, snow flurries had began to swirl, lightly coating the near-frozen earth, and the fire crackled inside the pot-bellied stove, warming the kitchen and dining room with heat from the sizzling ash and oak wood gathered for pre-winter days like this one and the cold winter to follow. Mr. Rhodes, having finished a second piece of pecan pie ("Just a sliver, please") leaned back in his chair, thanked Mother for the meal a third time, stretched slightly, peered over bifocals without rims, his watery blue eyes meeting my gaze, and asked, "What do you want to do after you finish school?" As always, he listened, this time to the indecisive, impromptu, unpolished verbiage of an average 11-year-old, taking it all in and finally saying, "You have time to decide." My Father, an honest, strong man, reminisced about his own life's choices, perhaps projecting feelings and thoughts of when he sat in my chair, and said, "I could have been a preacher, farmer, or a banker. All are honorable." Banks were trusted, and bankers were respected in those days.

SUMMARY

1. Communist-style government takeovers and closures of businesses make business assets and citizens' wealth vulnerable to theft or confiscation. Evidence is available that businesses have been seized without due process.

2. It is impractical for business managers to attempt to hedge their company from government seizures through normal protective measures. Bank secrecy and private business registration and asset-protection plans may provide for "self-insurance" against unlawful seizures.

3. Alternative currencies are becoming popular and are used by local, voluntarily participating businesses and individuals, even after the seizure of popular Liberty Dollar creator—Liberty Services—by the government.

4. Unsound monetary policy, through excess money from debt creation by non-asset backed, legal tender currency, has "stolen" purchasing power and the wealth of U.S. dollar holders.

5. Banks, brokers, states, and others have stolen or "frozen" customers' accounts.

6. The trust of banks and the respectability of bankers and other financial institutions continues to suffer.

Notes:

1. Mark Herpel, "NORFED Dissolved By the Board, 'Liberty Services' dba 'Liberty Dollar' Emerges," *American Chronicle,* quote by Andrew Williams cited in the article, December 28, 2006, http://www.americanchronicle.com/articles/view/18406.

2. Michael Webster, "Federal Government Closes Down Liberty Dollar," *Bonds Market,* July 16, 2010, http://bondsmarket.org/federal-government-closes-down-liberty-dollar.

3. Jacob C. Hornberger, "The Soviet-Style Attack on NORFED," The Future of Freedom Foundation, November 21, 2007, http://www.fff.org/comment/com0711j.asp.

4. Ibid.

5. Jeff Ignatius, "The Future of Money? With the Economy in a Wreck, Alternative Currencies Could Gain," *Berkshares, Inc.,* quote by Dan Priest, February 4, 2009, http://www.berkshares.org/press/09feb04.htm.

6. Ibid., Jacob C. Hornberger, http://www.fff.org/comment/com0711j.asp.

7. John Christian Ryter, "FBI Raids Liberty Dollar," *NewsWithViews.com,* November 17, 2007, http://www.newswithviews.com/Ryter/jon201.htm.

8. Free Talk Live, radio interview, Ian Freeman and Mark Edge, quote by Bernard von NotHause, November 17, 2007, http://letlibertyring.blogspot.com/2007/11/bernard-von-nothaus-on-free-talk-live.html.

9. Chris Powell, "Mistakenly Disclosed Affidavit Outlines Case Against Liberty Dollar," http://news.goldseek.com/GATA/1195420514.php, http://www.johnlocke.org/site-docs/meckdeck/pdfs/USAVLibdoll.pdf>, November 19, 2007.

10. John Christian Ryter, "F.B.I. Raids Liberty Dollar," *NewsWithViews.com,* November 17, 2007, http://webcache.googleusercontent.com/search?q=cache:PjP9GcQUN1IJ:www.newswithviews.com/Ryter/jon201.htm+fbi+raids+liberty+dollar+news+with+views&cd=4&hl=en&ct=clnk&gl=us.

11. Michael Webster, "Federal Government Closes Down Liberty Dollar," *Bonds Market,* July 16, 2010, *http://bondsmarket.org/federal-government-closes-down-liberty-dollar.*

12. Ryter, *NewsWithViews.*

13. Dan Shaw, "Liberty Dollar Maker, Three Others, Arrested by Feds," Evansville Courier & Press, June 5, 2009, http://www.courierpress.com/news/2009/jun/05/05web-LibertyDollar.

14. http:www.Berkshares.org.

15. http://www.digtriad.com/money/your_money/article.aspx?storyid=122045&catid=248.

16. http://www.modeldmedia.com/features/detroitcheers18809.aspx.

17. Alec MacGillis, "Federal Raid on Money Group Riles Ron Paul Supporters," *The Seattle Times,* quote by Jim Forsythe, November 17, 2007, http://seattletimes.nwsource.com/html/nationworld/2004019445_coins17.html.

18. Alan Greenspan, *Gold and Economic Freedom*, 1966, http://www.321gold.com/fed/greenspan/1966.html.

19. Ben White, "Bernanke Unwrapped," *The Washington Post*, November 15, 2005, http://www.washingtonpost.com/wp-dyn/content/article/2005/11/14/AR2005111401544.html.

20. Editor, Jim Rogers, "Bernanke Doesn't Know What He's Doing," *Wall Street Pit*, November 10, http://wallstreetpit.com/50092-jim-rogers-bernanke-doesnt-know-what-hes-doing.

21. Video, "Senator Sanders Goes Off on Bernanke," *YouTube.com*, March 3, 2009,http://www.youtube.com/watch?v=rCWXrMCGJT4&NR=1&feature=fvwp.

22. Video, "Alan Grayson: 'Which Foreigners Got the Fed's 500,000,000,000?' Bernanke: 'I Don't Know,'" *YouTube.com*, July 21, 2009, http://www.youtube.com/watch?v=n0NYBTkE1yQ&feature=related.

23. Kurt Nimmo, "Dollar Devaluation and Destruction of America Pick up Steam," July 11, 2010, http://www.infowars.com/dollar-devaluation-and-destruction-of-america-pick-up-steam.

24. G. Edward Griffin, *The Creature From Jekyll Island: A Second Look at the Federal Reserve*, Fourth Edition (Westlake Village, CA: American Media, 2002), 330

25. CBS News, quotation from website, June 17, 2009, http://www.cbsnews.com/stories/2009/06/17/politics/main5093719.shtml.

26. Ibid.

27. Elizabeth Leamy, "Not-So-Safe-Deposit Boxes: States Seize Citizens' Property to Balance Their Budgets," ABC News, Good Morning America, May 12, 2008, http://abcnews.go.com/GMA/story?id=4832471&page=1.

28. Ibid.

29. Ibid.

30. Ibid.

31. Ibid.

32. Rate it all, www.Rateitall.com, posted by Kuske, October 13, 2008, http://webcache.googleusercontent.com/search?q=cache:08AKgpIcyTAJ:www.rateitall.com/i-18935-etrade.aspx+e-trade+steals+money+from+customers&cd=21&hl=en&ct=clnk&gl=us.

33. Ibid., Posted by Aryan0301, February 24, 2008

34. Ibid., Posted by Stockpro, November 21, 2007

35. Naomi Wolf, "Banks Siding Against the Customer in Fraud Cases," *The Huffington Post*, August, August 23, 2010, http://www.huffingtonpost.com/naomi-wolf/post_722_b_691188.html.

36. Ibid.

37. Elizabeth Dunbar, "Former Wells Fargo Bank Teller Charged with Stealing 100K," Minnesota Public Radio, August 6, 2010, http://minnesota.publicradio.org/display/web/2010/08/06/former-wells-fargo-teller-charged-with-stealing-100k.

38. Ibid.

39. Dan Goodin, "IT Insider Admits Stealing Info For 2,000 Bank Employees: Makes Off With 1.1 M," *The Register,* July 2, 2010, http://www.theregister. co.uk/2010/07/02/bank_insider_data_theft.

40. Ibid.

41. Supreme Court of the State of New York, County of New York: NAOMI WOLF v. JPMORGAN CHASE & CO., INDEX NO. 651288/2010, August 17, 2010, http://i.cdn.turner.com/dr/teg/tsg/release/sites/default/files/assets/ naomiwolfcomplaint.pdf.

42. Alan Gathright, "Bank Officer Accused of Stealing $1 Million From Widow," *Denver News,* http://www.thedenverchannel.com/news/21946280/detail. html.

43. Ibid.

♦ TWO ♦

Stolen Freedoms

"Freedom is first of all a responsibility before the God from whom we come."

—Alan Keyes, Political Activist and Presidential Candidate

NEW WORLD ORDER PRIVACY INVASIONS

Police sirens scream, and helicopters hover above telephone lines, as unmarked cars speed silently by with their portable red lights flashing. Terrified citizens stand on their lawns looking overhead, or they peer out through worn screen doors or from upstairs bedroom windows. Some take cover in back rooms or basements. All are terrified. A neighborhood search is on. No one knows who is being hunted.

Door to door, uniformed and plain-clothed enforcers demand entry into the homes of schoolteachers, bus drivers, ironworkers, carpenters, janitors, salesmen, doctors, and clerks. One man refuses to open the door unless a proper search warrant issued by a judge is presented; entry into his flat is immediately forced. He is beaten, handcuffed, and transported away. No others ask questions, as their homes, garages, attics, and yards are searched, amidst the noisy radios and industry-coded chatter.

All residents present identification papers and give personal and business information to masked, unidentified soldiers of the state, without resistance.

Handguns' serial numbers are run through databases accessed with laptops that provide real-time verification of registration or lack of proper state documentation. Weapons without proper licenses are confiscated, as are an illegal SKS and two short-barreled shotguns. Two neighborhood residents are questioned at length, once their hidden money safes are discovered, and are told a state-assigned accountant will later interview them to determine the legality of the cash and assess the probable tax liability. Several identification documents are scrutinized, photocopied, and will be checked through INTERPOL the following day. Other property, deemed contraband, is discovered and seized as evidence; arrests are made.

CENSOR-US DATABANK

Proprietary government software screened masses of people and their owned and rented properties. A computer printout produced their names, identifying information, medical and employment histories, credit bureau reports, and criminal records of flagged resident-suspects, based on "abnormal" histories and living habits.

The computer spit out data, including unusually high utility bills, certain credit card activities, large changes in bank account balances, high-dollar ammunition purchases, credit rating changes, and other criteria designed to track the targeted citizens.

Big Bureaucrat's supercomputer program is designed to ferret out terrorists, tax delinquents, alimony skippers, drug dealers, parole violators, unlawful gun owners, money launderers, deadbeat dads, fraudulent bankrupts, phony insurance claimants, debtors in arrears, and others who owe or are suspected of owing a government agency or corporation partner.

Corporations and government resources have been merged to enforce civil and criminal laws.

FREEDOM LIFESTYLE

I know how to keep my liberty and privacy, as people and patriots everywhere relinquish theirs and believe certain media talking heads who claim citizens must let government know where they live, work, travel, and keep their money—all in the name of whatever national guise is the order of the era. I believe none of it.

My home, job, automobile, personal possessions, investments, and money are the results of my risks, studies, efforts, and labors. I am educated, and I know the law. My founding fathers promised me privacy as they wrote the United States Constitution, and I am under no obligation to let others—especially government, my employees—dictate to me and steal my liberty by invading my professional and personal privacy.

A truly free society does not trade personal privacy for government support and subsidies or let bureaucrats and "soldiers of the state" track them as they travel, bank, work, and live. My government is under my employ. I am their boss, and I do not compromise my constitutional rights or my value system.

I demand my freedom, and I practice privacy.

I have a duty to follow the laws of the land, and I have an obligation to demand the same of my government. And I do.

My family has a home that will not be discovered through county property record searches or utility company databases. Our family members' credit reports are locked to the outside world, and we will not give up the keys: not to banks, credit card companies, landladies or landlords, employers, phone companies, utility service clerks, bankers, real estate brokers, state agencies, salespeople, or customers' men.

We value our privacy and avoid all who might want to stalk my teenage daughter, steal my wife's jewelry collection, heist my identity, hack into my son's computer, or vandalize our home. We systematically prevent the world from knowing the whereabouts of our house, jobs, property, investments, money, and automobiles. We are a privacy team who believe our freedoms to be ours, and we do not tolerate privacy invasions from anyone. And we are ready and prepared.

CONTROLLERS OF MONEY AND PRIVACY

My role models taught me responsibility. I learned to work, think, read, and ask questions long before now-popular movies, articles, and books exposed the Federal Reserve System as a private corporation formed to create fiat money for the benefit of a few, while destroying the wealth of most, primarily through the loss of purchasing power for essential goods and services.

I do not believe the great inflation lie. Educated businesspeople understand that units of value have a consistent means of exchange, while the currency of choice is merely a receipt for a true "store of value" that has credibility in the marketplace.

Our dollars have been devalued, debased, printed, or issued as digital credits in such massive amounts that the world has recognized the scam that is the dilution of money values, for the sake of immediate credit. These credits are usually motivated by greed. Policies set by the money-issuers and their government teammates are unsound, economi-cally unfeasible fix-attempts for certain "preferred customers"—mainly motivated by political favors owed, bailouts of cronies' companies, or outright thievery, all to be paid for by the debtors without choice—the residents and citizens of the once-great United States of America.

A debt has been created that is now mathematically impossible to repay—except through yet more serious currency devaluation. The di-lution of money value is so serious that it is unlikely the U.S. dollar will remain the reserve currency of the world in future years.

A money system and monetary policy are closely correlated to free-dom and privacy. For without a sound, stable, honest monetary system, no hope remains for freedom to build wealth and prosper; there is only perpetual debt backed by human collateral—salaried slaves and spend-ers of currency being devalued at rapid rates.

The benefactors of a monetary system lacking a value-backed sys-tem of assets, a non-asset based currency, was created out of the sham that is the Federal Reserve System. This "lie of value" enables a few to prosper through massive "credit earnings," and though in reality a false-hood, it is spendable for wealth creation in pyramided dollars.

The human collateral—"sheeple," property of their instant wealth-creation masters—must be kept under watch, lest they escape the cor-ral of slavery imposed upon them to keep the pyramid scheme of phony dollars afloat. Their once-private affairs must become the business of the state for collection of stored labor due—work taxed from gross re-ceipts and "taxation" through money devaluation—the horrible side ef-fects of irresponsible, criminal, unsound money creation.

INTENDED CONSEQUENCES

The issuers of money from debt enter more dollars into circulation, and they have no choice but to dictate to the masses if they want to continue the irresponsible monetary fraud that is the U.S. dollar—cre-ated from debt rather than intrinsic value.

The Federal Reserve System, the central bank of the United States of America, was created by a private group of financiers and became law under the Federal Reserve Act passed in 1913. The Federal Reserve was created in secret on Jekyll Island, Georgia[1] and gave control of the U.S. monetary system to private bankers. The secret trip to Jekyll Island, where the "Fed" was created, was cited by Frank Vanderlip in his auto-biography, *From Farmboy to Financier:*

"Our secret expedition to Jekyll Island was the occasion of the actual conception of what eventually became the Federal Reserve System, The essential points of the Aldrich Plan were all contained in the Federal Reserve Act as it was passed."[2]

Only seven men attended this secret meeting where the Federal Reserve System was conceived, and these men's wealth "represented an estimated one-fourth of the total wealth of the entire world."[3]

The men who attended the Jekyll Island meeting were:

"1. Nelson W. Aldrich, Republican "Whip" in the Senate, Chairman of the National Monetary Commission, and father-in-law to John D. Rockefeller, Jr.

2. Henry P. Davison, Senior Partner of J. P. Morgan Company.

3. Charles D. Norton, President of the 1st National Bank of New York.

4. A. Piatt Andrew, Assistant Secretary of the Treasury.

5. Frank A. Vanderlip, President of the National City Bank of New York, representing William Rockefeller.

6. Benjamin Strong, head of J. P. Morgan's Bankers Trust Company, later to become head of the System.

7. Paul M. Warburg, a partner in Kuhn, Loeb & Company, representing the Rothchilds and Warburgs in Europe."[4]

The government bureaucrat-contractors with the Federal Reserve System have to steal the freedom and privacy of the masses in order to control the many who, through more legislative scams, will become the victims of the powerful greed-lords and be forced into becoming more indentured servitude-salary slaves, given allowances only once government's piece of the "wage pie" is taken and redistributed. Government's slice is taken from the talented and skilled, the risk takers, the workaholics, the lucky, the rich by inheritance and given to the underachievers, the young, the illegal aliens, and the unmotivated—all designed to fatten the "sheeple" in order to perpetuate the power of a government out of control.

WITHOUT REPRESENTATION

Your current rulers have facilitated the bastardizing of the monetary system for selfish, unconscionable reasons—usually with money, control, and political motivations as their driving forces rather than the good of their constituents and the preservation of their country's Constitution, which they have sworn to uphold.

Government officials at the highest levels are the partners of corporate benefactors and are the fascist-like invaders of countries with conjured-up dangers, most improbable and unproven and sold to people—or "sheeple"—who believe that someone else, by title, authority, right, or official designation, has the power to tell them what to do without rational accountability.

MASS HERD MENTALITY

The masses do not know the source of their money. Like sheep, they are branded with Social Security Numbers, corralled, and held captive with low-salaried jobs and paid with diluted dollars. They have their freedom and privacy attacked by their predator-masters, through higher sales taxes, a promised state-sponsored health program, and the ever-present and intolerable loss of purchasing power of the dollars they are forced to use as a means of exchange for essential goods and services and numerous taxes at every state, local, and national level.

To be uneducated and incapable of critical thinking is horrible. Because of ignorance of the monetary system and the central bank of the United States, the Federal Reserve System, the public is unable to perceive the present reality. Meanwhile, government strives to control citizens' lives in their quest for total control through collection of tax receipts, property seizures, and imprisonments necessary to assure that the debt machine is kept running at full throttle.

The money creators have to perpetuate the fraud by continuously buying and bonding with "representatives" of the people to ensure more bondage—slavery for all worker bees to fund the debt-induced monetary system, without assets backing the spendable cash. This system is irrational, a fairy tale, a business misnomer—money without value and with no backing by a basket of commodities, land, minerals in the ground, or gold in the bank. Instead, the system is perpetuated and assured through the collateral of the payers of tax and losers of their purchasing power, privacy, and freedoms, who are penalized through a continuing lower standard of living, and all to fund the most gigantic thievery ever—a criminal enterprise, to be certain, and without question. Hidden or overt, it is taxation without representation. And the public accepts it, through ignorance and passivity.

DEBTOR SLAVES

The Federal Reserve System is fraud by definition and the textbook example of a Ponzi scheme—irrational, unsound, immoral, unethical, nonsensical pyramiding that even a bright third grader would not buy, were he given the chance to decide. Yet the typical American knows not the source of his true trouble: money, not controlled by himself but by a powerful machine that promises to steal more of his freedom and privacy. Fiat money, if it is to be repaid to the slave masters who issued it, requires line workers' debt payments without fail or default.

Your monetary system is ruined. Your country is lost. Your privacy is the target of the predators who feed the debt machine as they recruit new debtors en masse to join the current salary slaves. Never mind immigration laws, the illegal aliens are indeed valuable as cheap laborers and automatic debtors and are being groomed as the system's newest salary slaves—as sheep being branded and corralled, then prepared by "fattening" them for the financial and freedom slaughter happening today.

FREEDOM ACTOR

How does one escape the corral and regain freedom in a country and world gone mad? Who are you? It starts with a willingness to learn, a desire to jump the fence, scoot between the barbed wire, or slip through the gate and break free—the right way, legally, while protecting yourself and your loved ones.

More and more people have been alerted to the losses of freedom and privacy today than in previous years. America is at a point of desperation. Will she survive? That should not be your concern, entirely. First, take care of you and yours. Politicians cannot be coaxed or changed, but you can be as free as you wish—all while practicing high-level privacy as you travel, bank, work, and live in your corner of the universe. And you can do it while following the laws of your particular jurisdiction. To ever break laws for the sake of privacy is neither necessary nor advisable—it defeats the purpose. Besides, you are afforded your rights to privacy by the United States Constitution. Do not forget it.

You can tap into privacy principles, techniques, and resources created to enable you to make your business and personal money and assets invisible to those who want to track, trace, and take from you. Through planning, study, diligence, and the intelligent use of the practice of privacy, you can develop your awareness to the fullest extent, and your new knowledge base and well-honed communication skills will enable you to win any battle for privacy and freedom you face today and in future years.

Throughout my writings on the subject of privacy, I continuously stress the point that it matters greatly how an individual approaches the job of obtaining services and goods. Pat answers to questions about privacy are seldom the end of the task itself. For instance, one person may quickly breeze through the process of establishing a relationship with a service, enabling him to cash business checks because he followed procedures and communicated to the right people at the company, all while providing minimal information—much less than would be required at the local bank. Someone else, with less planning under her belt and without the right contacts at the company, coupled with less effective communication skills, may struggle to accomplish the same or a similar objective.

One should understand such differences in effectiveness between individuals in their efforts to obtain bank secrecy and financial privacy. This is the case because differences exist in the people you deal with or in a given institution, as well as in your requirements and communication skills. Learning to understand the *freedom attitude,* as well as how the public reacts to privacy invasions and government and corporate propaganda generally, will provide a foundation for favorable results when one is faced with the tasks of finding what they need. Likewise, awareness of the behavior of the masses who allow themselves to be told what to do, without resistance in most cases, provides foundational work for thought and privacy planning.

Who are you? It matters a great deal. This is the focus of the next chapter.

SUMMARY

1. Considerable danger for loss of freedoms exists for those dependent on government.

2. Living as the masses assures the risk of conflict as police state powers increase, even as freedoms are stolen. Few choose to demand their rights to freedom and privacy, as afforded them by the United States Constitution.

3. Certain families live, travel, work, and bank beneath the radar as a matter of personal and business policy, to assure freedom from criminals, identity thieves, stalkers and other privacy intrusions. All laws should and can be followed when living a high-level privacy lifestyle.

4. A fraudulent monetary system is in place in the United States of America. The Federal Reserve System, a private corporation, controls monetary policy as per the Federal Reserve Act of 1913. Your government does not control your money, and the U.S. dollar's purchasing power has steadily depreciated as Americans' wealth has been stolen and destroyed through this unsound, fraudulent, money-from-debt policy.

5. Governmental theft of freedom and privacy assures that citizens are forced into participating as debtors, while their "representatives" do not abide by the majority's desire. Your government has stolen freedoms and privacy in order to track and trace the money and wealth of citizens, as they are forced to pay the greatest tax of all—mistakenly and commonly known as inflation—the devaluation of the U.S. dollar. This loss of purchasing power is the fault of greedy politicians and their corporate co-conspirators, who created debt out of nothing, thereby creating more debt and an oversupply of dollars or credits of dollars for the purpose of immediate funding for many illegitimate endeavors, without accountability and the approval of citizens.

6. The once-strong U.S. dollar is a ruined currency, long term, due to the irresponsible, excessive creation of fiat money. The U.S. has sunken into being a hopeless debtor nation without meaningful productivity, largely because of irresponsible government and pseudo-government

agencies. These are mainly the choice of representatives who rule without rational policy but instead kowtow to funders of their campaigns and continue to create debt as a source of funds for operations, while forcing citizens without representation to participate as payers of the debt through the hidden tax of dollar devaluation.

7.   Citizens who choose to be free have the right to develop a freedom and privacy plan that assures their continued freedom, while keeping their natural, God-given, and constitutional rights

NOTES:

1.   Eustace Mullins, *Secrets of the Federal Reserve: The London Connection,* First Edition (Staunton, VA: Bankers Research Institute, 1983), 9.

2.   Ibid.

3.   G. Edward Griffin, *The Creature From Jekyll Island: A Second Look at the Federal Reserve,* Fourth Edition (Westlake Village, CA: American Media, 2002), 24.

4.   Ibid.

THREE

Who Are You?

"Relying on the government to protect your privacy is like asking a peeping tom to install your window blinds."
—John Perry Barlow, Political Activist

PERSONAL ASSESSMENT

How do the masses respond, when disaster events provide a rationale for government to destroy privacy rights and basic freedoms? Sadly, they generally do as they are told and *when* they are told to do it.

Your attitudes and beliefs will influence how objective and assertive you will be, as you absorb news events and respond to new policies implemented by corporations and government in their attempts to track and trace you, your property, and your money.

An awareness of what is happening today, combined with objective, critical thinking will enable you to make choices and thwart the efforts of those wishing to have access to your entire life.

Money privacy is an essential component of basic freedoms, though this is seemingly not realized or understood by the public. Exceptions exist, of course. Some people still value their freedom and insist on privacy rights.

GRANDDAD

Granddad had only a few years of formal education. However, he could read newspapers, debate politics, build houses, weld professionally, manage a business, and speak two languages. He saw the Vietnam War for the fraud he believed it was from the very beginning.

"We don't belong over there. The bankers make money when we fight wars," he explained. Granddad believed wars were unnecessary. His heritage proved it.

"The Swiss haven't fought a war in nearly 600 years."

How could that be, I wondered? As a young boy, I already knew people who had fought in three recent wars in which my own country had participated. I continued to wonder and think about what Granddad had said. Were wars *really* unnecessary?

Freedom was a passion for Granddad—a living right he taught me to claim, not as a flag-waving citizen, but as a human with God-given rights. And of course, privacy is a part of our constitutional rights, and I was taught early on about the importance of that, as well.

Asking someone about their money and business was a big no-no in our family, and I believe this money secrecy was passed down to the family from the long-standing Swiss banking secrecy traditions that today are crumbling, due to pressure from the United States military-industrial complex. Still, I practice today the bank secrecy policies of my ancestors, through innovations pieced together by way of legal entities, privacy-friendly businesses, and money-control methods designed to prevent anyone—government included—from taking what is mine or yours through court orders, confiscations, seizures, or theft.

This is doable even today, amidst the verbiage of the media puppets—those talking heads who promise you that your privacy is a thing of the past and that you are obliged to offer your business secrets and money-holding information to the state for national security, to prevent another 9/11, to help win the war on drugs, or whatever other pretext the regime in power wants to shout at you. Believe none of it. Your business is *your* business.

PRIVACY CHOICES

I am on record as saying that Americans and others today have a greater opportunity to build a more totally free and private lifestyle today than in previous decades. The reason for these relatively unknown freedom opportunities is that more entrepreneurial companies with innovative management continue to see an increased demand for the privacy lifestyle, as folks like you and me demand it and exercise both our God-given and promised constitutional rights to claim these freedoms. Along with this demand comes the supply to satisfy the demand for privacy goods and services, as businesses and businesspeople work to accommodate the needs of the privacy advocate and as an increased amount of information becomes available to those who want it.

Today, you do indeed have the power to insist that your privacy rights be respected, and I hope you will learn to exercise these rights, as you protect your money and yourself from any number of privacy invasions.

PROTECT YOUR "SELF"

One characteristic of higher-level "thinking animals" is the ability to develop the self-esteem that provides the necessary confidence to allow one to become unique. As people are individuals, they separate themselves from others, no matter how subtle this separation, and develop the ability to reason and make choices. An important part of this human growth and development process is insistence on personal privacy.

When you are asked to give your Social Security Number to a medical doctor's front office clerk, do you provide it? How about when you go to the dentist? The dental service patient form is going to be similar to the one you filled out prior to seeing the medical doctor.

When you allow others to control you through obtaining identifiers and other privacy invasions without a rational cause or reason, you lose a portion of your sense of *self* and become like "non-thinking" animals that are branded, herded, and prepared to be slaughtered.

I expect that you do provide your Social Security Number to front-office personnel, part-time clerks who sometimes work in medical and dental offices, and others you deem to represent those who have an "official" status and have a right to this highly sensitive identifier—but you should not, in my opinion. In fact, it may be a costly mistake if you do.

It was expensive for Joe Ryan, whose name and Social Security Number were used by a convict treated at a hospital that sent the real Ryan a $44,000 bill for the hospital treatment.[1]

Criminals gravitate toward wherever the money can be located, and frequently, individuals' personal and confidential information—their name, date of birth, home address, home telephone number, and especially their Social Security Number—provides a clear road map for the thief to steal a person's valuable data and property. That person may then become the target of other identity thieves or criminals. And since you have no control over how businesses, government agencies, medical practices, banks, stock brokerage firms, and dental offices secure your private information, it is best to refuse to provide your most sensitive data to them in the first place, whenever practical to do so.

Are you worried about bucking the system just a bit or drawing attention to yourself? How about refusing to do business with a financial services company—a bank, a stockbroker, or a check-cashing service—when their part-time clerk/acting "manager" insists on grabbing your Social Security Number and placing it in their database for thousands of other part-timers to view and perhaps even steal? Are you shy about refusing to provide a thumbprint to the nice senior clerk who sneers at you through the plate glass window down at the bank, when you question bank policies? Thinking about refusing to give that nice new orthodontist your Social Security Number, too? Why do dentists' clerks think they need patients' Social Security Numbers?

Often, it is most prudent to avoid the behavior of the masses and stand up for your beliefs and privacy rights. Approximately 200 dental patients in Denver, Colorado, were apparently too trusting of their dental providers when these crucial records were left in a car that was stolen. Two men were reportedly charged with identity theft.[2]

I never provide my Social Security Number to anyone or any business *unless* it is required by law to do so *or* unless the service is so valuable for me that I believe it to be worth the risk, and I cannot obtain the service without providing my SSN.

I have not memorized my Social Security Number, so it is impossible for me to give it to government agents or law enforcement if I were asked to do so without prior notice. Certain individuals have been asked for these identifiers during routine traffic stops or other investigations in the field, as police and others attempt to gather all the information possible on their subjects during these investigations.

I believe everyone should cooperate fully with law enforcement, while making certain to demand their constitutional rights be respected and never abused.

Would you provide a policeman with a blood sample? I expect many who are not in the know—or who are too drunk to know the difference when asked—would allow a medical technician from law enforcement to draw their blood, but this is a horrible invasion of privacy, in my opinion. Think of the abuse that could occur if someone had access to the laboratory results of any number of people. These procedures have reportedly been used on drunk drivers or those accused of being intoxicated. The drunk driver or those accused of this offense are ᴄᴀᴅ͵ prey for cops and are being milked by the system—and rightfully so—to a certain degree, *if and when* they are found guilty.

How about being forced to take swine flu vaccinations or other immunizations deemed necessary by the state? Do you consent to having your school-aged children vaccinated? The masses generally do whatever they are told to do by someone perceived to have a position of authority, or who represents themselves as an "agent" of someone who *does* have a position of authority. And the likelihood is high for consent of the masses to the dictates of Big Bureaucrat, when mandates are for health reasons, and especially for the health of the children.

Clerks who take "applications" of prospective new patients for doctors are "agents" for doctors, and bankers who tell you to provide your Social Security Number and home address to them if you want a bank account are "agents" for the Federal Reserve System's owners and for the Internal Revenue Service—both masters of the masses. The cell telephone companies that require you to provide them with access to your credit bureau files are "agents" for government regulatory agencies that monitor citizens' phone conversations and easily identify them by matching cell phone numbers and records with the account holder of record.

New patients who advise clerks that they do not have their SSN memorized and who shield this identifier from medical offices and the like, while negotiating with supervisors who waive the application or form requirement, succeed in keeping their privacy.

Privacy seekers who use company bank accounts with anonymous Employer Identification Numbers and keep their Social Security Numbers off of bank records—or who instead use check-cashing services for clearing company or personal checks without providing SSNs—retain their privacy, as well.

Those who do not want their names associated with telephone records or bills avoid land-line telephones, except pay telephones and selected third-party phones, and instead buy cell phones with cash, load them with prepaid phone cards purchased with cash, and avoid having their privacy invaded by part-time clerks and others who work at cell phone retail outlets.

Privacy living is a mindset. It is a lifestyle developed through an awareness of independence and responsibility and a belief system that protects personal and business information and holds one's right to privacy in the highest regard, without interference from individuals or businesses, and especially not from government.

Recognize the differences between lifestyles of the masses versus living as an informed, decision-making, free-thinking individual. Freedom thinkers avoid the privacy invasions given up so easily by the majority of the population, and they must necessarily expend more time, effort, and money to retain their privacy. And it is worth every minute, every ounce of energy, and every nickel it costs to do it.

MASS DEPENDENCE

While standing in line waiting to pay for items purchased in a drug store, I could not help but overhear a conversation between the pharmacist and a customer.

"What's your 'social,' Ms. Smith?" asked Mr. Pharmacist. She blurted it out with no more hesitation than if she were ordering a hamburger at a fast food restaurant, and at three times the decibel level. All in my line up to fifteen feet away heard her loudly announce the most important identifier this woman has, and someone may have memorized it. And the masses wonder why an identity theft occurs every few seconds. Or why the crime of stalking has become an epidemic. Or why business identity thefts are on the upswing. Do *not* give your most important identifier, the Social Security Number, to anyone or any entity unless it is required by law or absolutely necessary for you to do so. Even then, be discreet about it.

The masses dislike thinking or going against the proverbial grain and instead opt for the line of least resistance. You will find, in your quest for privacy, especially high-level financial privacy, that you will be put to the back of the line, placed on hold for near-indefinite periods, hung up on, and discouraged from doing it anyway, except according to "Ms. Clerk III's" way. And that "way" is based on a manual-doctrine often compiled by some Big Bureaucrat in his ivory tower and designed to track and trace you, your business, your assets and money, and all associated with you, until you are a part of a giant data bank—one that can be accessed with a finger click by part-timers and pawns of the power-hungry corporate-government marriage partners in America today, the dictionary-perfect definition of fascism.

Your first task will be to recognize that *privacy is freedom*. And the masses do not have freedom. In fact, when someone can track and trace another through any number of control mechanisms (databases) in place and available to many who claim control, this is the textbook example of a citizenry under total control of government and certain "authorized" segments of the private sector as well—to say nothing of others who can afford the subscription fees to purchase personal and confidential information held in these data banks.

Why should you be able to be traced to your place of employment? Whose business is it where you store your money or what real property or other property you own? Who on earth has the right to know the driver's name of an automobile simply by accessing the records of the license plate number? And why in the world would anyone make their home address records available to an accessible database?

Free people, truly free people, demand their freedom and privacy for the protection it provides themselves and their families against any number of unwanted intrusions—identity theft, property theft, stalkers, government intrusions, and other potentially dangerous privacy invasions.

How can you avoid an invasion of your personal privacy and freedom? You must educate yourself far beyond what you were taught in public schools, colleges, and universities and read and study the works of those who provide information on how the world *really* works. You must learn to think outside the box, so to speak, and recognize the true motivations driving the behaviors of those who claim to rule over you.

How you think is important as you exercise your freedom, and regaining your privacy is a huge part of being free.

CONFLICTING MATERIAL INTERESTS

Many in the population have a self-interest in conforming to the whims of Big Bureaucrats, since from them, they receive salary checks, pension benefits, welfare checks, and subsidy payments, or are dependent on a family member who receives such funds. Money, the potential of being given a prestigious job or keeping one's present job, and/or the likelihood of a promotion or other career opportunity tend to sway the thinking of totally rational people at times. Evidence of this is seen in recent examples of irrational thinking, expressions, and conclusions concerning certain serious and life-changing happenings in the United States of America.

The country of Iraq was invaded, though the U.S. president at that time, George W. Bush, admitted on camera during an interview with news personnel that the Iraqis had nothing to do with the events of 9/11, and he further admitted there were never any weapons of mass destruction found, even though these weapons were claimed by U.S. government officials to be in the possession of Saddam Hussein prior to the invasion of Iraq in March 2003.[3]

"Not finding weapons of mass destruction in Iraq—the reason Bush gave for the Iraqi invasion—was a pretty serious matter."[4]

Indeed, and one criminal attorney, Vincent Bugliosi, has called for the prosecution of George W. Bush for murder and has devoted an entire book to the subject. Bugliosi advises, "What is recommended in this book is, as the title says, the prosecution of the president of the United States for murder."[5]

The "official" reason for the Twin Towers' collapse on September 11, 2001 was fire that had such extremely hot temperatures that three steel-framed buildings fell into their own footprints at near free-fall speed and turned to dust after only two of these buildings were hit by airplanes. This story has no rational basis and is neither supported by basic laws of physics nor by scientific evidence. Professor Steven Jones' paper suggests the buildings were brought down by controlled demolition.[6]

Building number 7—the 47-story building located several hundred feet away from the Twin Towers—was never hit by a plane, yet it too collapsed into its own footprint, as demolished buildings do, and the decision was admittedly made to "pull it" (a controlled demolition term) according to statements made during an interview with lease-holder Larry Silverstein.[7]

Building number 7 was not mentioned in the official 9/11 commission report, and Silverstein was not investigated for his comments. Of course, each of these happenings would be key pieces of evidence *if* an objective and real criminal investigation were conducted by professional, dedicated criminal investigators whose goal was to obtain the true facts of the biggest crime on U.S. soil in the history of the country. The official report is obviously false to those with the objective thinking capability to separate themselves from the irrational conclusions fed to them by the government officials' reports and certain media sources.

These cases are examples of "mass dependence" thinking and irrational reasoning and are cited to enlighten you as to what is possible when this mass dependence is at least partially responsible for converting normal "thinking animals" into sheep through the influence of authority-type figures (a government's official story) with conflicting material interests.

We cannot depend on our government to work in our best interest at any level whatsoever. Today, we have to listen to certain Internet radio talk show hosts and the interviews of credible researchers and read the works of authors of books and articles who sometimes risk everything for the sake of truth. Any person has to have the capacity for independent, unbiased thinking, while avoiding the temptation of material dependence and comfort—or promised comfort—in exchange for selling out, for whatever reason. Let's not kid ourselves. We are all human, and when one is afforded comforts in exchange for looking the other way or for "going along with the program" while not making waves, it is the rare individual who can do the right thing and sacrifice it all, or most of it, for "right's sake."

If you are a believer in freedom and want to dedicate yourself to obtaining what is rightfully yours, naturally and constitutionally, you may simply work toward opting out of what most people never question. You can, for the most part, learn to live beneath the radar and travel, bank, work, and live anonymously. Study, learn, and demand your freedom through self reliance and a "self insurance" plan that will protect you against the giant octopus of corporate and government privacy invaders that grab for every bit of your personal and confidential information and attempt to invade every facet of your life. How you think is everything. Think freedom—and dedicate yourself to living without a master.

FREEDOM INSTINCTS

If you are "captive" of the huge corporate/government machine and believe you have little or no freedom or privacy, but you want to gain your true independence, I urge you to begin to study and learn how to live privately, based on your personal and business requirements, during these modern times. This can be accomplished through practices that assure you freedom, even as the masses continue to bow and kowtow to a few who promise their protection from questionable threats, while Big Bureaucrat continues dictating his selfish agenda.

Do not confuse a healthy desire for freedom with antisocial behavior. Freedom seekers work within the system and obey the rule of law, while the antisocial personality ignores the law. Your goal, as one who desires a privacy living lifestyle, should be to accomplish *all* of your privacy objectives, while following every law in your given jurisdiction. Be prepared to spend more time, effort, and money than the masses as you accomplish your desired freedom levels without breaking laws. In fact, it is not necessary to break laws in your quest for privacy living. The breaking of laws would defeat the purpose of privacy entirely and place your freedom, the heart of the privacy lifestyle, at risk.

KNOWLEDGE BASE

I grew up reading a series of privacy books written for entertainment more than for the practical application of privacy principles. Buried within these chapters were vague ideas about new citizenship in far-away lands, hidden business structures in offshore havens, and temporary locations on multiple continents. It was a fun fantasy, but true and correct answers to my unspoken questions were few and far between. I found the authors to have a foundational knowledge about the subject of privacy, but their answers were not do-able for most of us because of the limitations of resources and tolerance for the lifestyle exemplified by the wanderer subject-model of the books. In fact, I learned to appreciate the literature, while acknowledging that the purpose of the books was not for instruction on how to implement this independent, private lifestyle—at least not entirely.

The truth is that most privacy seekers do not have the knowledge base, let alone the motivation, to reduce their profiles for successful privacy living. High-level privacy living is a systematic endeavor built on a foundation of privacy principles and concepts that are proven to withstand the privacy invasive inquiries that would pierce the veils of the personal privacy of 99.9 percent of the masses. In order to gain a high level of privacy in your personal life and in your career, you will be required first to learn how to find available resources for your privacy needs, and then to develop the motivation to succeed in living beneath the radar, to whatever degree you so choose.

PRIVACY BASICS

Barring an unnatural or dangerous privacy invasion, you will normally begin to enhance your privacy over a period of time. As a certain level of privacy becomes fashionable, due to the media hype about the problems and costs of identity theft or the dangers of a criminal stalker, you will naturally gravitate toward a certain level of "acceptable" privacy living. You will be encouraged by the talking heads—employees of the "masters" and Big Bureaucrat—to turn over your personal and confidential information to trusted third parties in exchange for your "safety."

Of course, your police force, government agencies, private credit bureaus, banks, brokerage companies, landladies and lords, utility service providers, insurance companies, and others expect to have a right to all of your personal and business information, and just as the sheep exchange their freedom for their payment of grain to satisfy their palate needs, the masses give up their freedom (privacy and self) in exchange for necessary services.

In fact, a huge part of freedom is the privacy to travel, bank, work, and live anonymously while following the law, no matter how unfair a given statute may seem. It is your responsibility to abide by every law while keeping your freedom and living a privacy lifestyle at whatever level you so desire.

Who has the right to your privacy and God-given liberty—the freedom to think and live as you wish so long as you do not infringe on or harm others? No one has the right to your business unless you give it to them. And those who have the least right of all are strangers, whether they are governmental authority-type figures, or criminals seeking to unseat you from your property or freedom.

By obtaining proven privacy living principles and concepts, you can develop a workable knowledge base and make the necessary adjustments, whether simple or drastic, to ensure that your desired level of privacy is accomplished.

RESOURCES FOR THE RESOURCEFUL

A middle-aged man approached me after an evening seminar had ended and requested my signature on the seminar program schedule and again on the book. Dressed in jeans and a T-shirt and wearing sunglasses, I noticed during our conversation that he hadn't made much use of *Privacy Crisis* and expected he wanted pat answers to some of the more complicated questions concerning high-level privacy living.

"Where can I open a bank account without giving them my Social Security Number?" he asked. I've probably been asked that question several thousand times over the past few years, in person and in e-mail and mail correspondences.

"What do you want to accomplish with your financial privacy plan?" I responded. He did not have a definite answer and had not thought about his goals and objectives. He had not defined what he wanted and had no plan of action. Nor had he studied.

Generally, people expect to do very little themselves and believe that experts who write about a given field have all the answers. Resources are available to those who will seek them out, but a list of lenient banks that waive tax identifiers is not available anywhere, as far as I know. I uested that the aforementioned gentleman explain his banking needs, which were rather uncomplicated, and advised him to review the section on *Finances*—and follow that review with an in-depth review and study of the *Behavior* section—of *Privacy Crisis: Identity Theft Prevention Plan and Guide to Anonymous Living.* Then I explained the importance of defining one's privacy requirements and the value of practicing communication to successfully negotiate for these requirements.

FREEDOM AND PRIVACY LIVING

The home address of the Alex Corbin family cannot be found in any database. Their automobile's registration name, "The Copper River Valley Irrevocable Trust," cannot be traced to the primary drivers, Alex and his wife, Shirley. The telephones used by the Corbin family are wireless devices purchased at retail stores over the counter and without privacy-invasive subscription information. Minutes to these cell phones are replenished as needed through the purchase of telephone calling cards that, like the cell phones, are purchased with cash.

Money orders are purchased as needed for the payment of household bills, and the cash to purchase these money orders is withdrawn and recorded as a "draw" on the business account of the Family Limited Partnership—an anonymous holding or the Limited Liability Company that owns a retail, e-commerce website controlled by Mr. and Mrs. Corbin.

There is no mortgage on the family residence—a two-story, four-bedroom, two-bath home located in a Western city. The employment databases do not hold information on Alex or Shirley, co-managers of the aforementioned limited partnership and LLC. Nor is Mrs. Corbin's consultation business available in databases, as the company that receives payment for her services is an LLC registered anonymously and utilizing the Trust Manager Principle.[8]

You can defeat the machines designed to control your life through information gathering—and the dangerous human predators, as well—when you dedicate yourself to the task of learning the ropes of successful anonymous living.

One of your greatest challenges will be to secure your financial privacy—an important component of privacy living. In spite of the changes in "secret offshore havens" in the last few years, one can still maintain high-level financial privacy. And though the principles and concepts I have used to gain these privacy advantages are different than you will find *anywhere* in print, these methods—and there are a number of them—are proven to work during attempts made to invade the money and financial privacy of those desiring to keep their hard-earned assets under their control without the risk of seizure or confiscation. These topics are the subject of the following chapters.

SUMMARY

1. True freedom involves the use of money and asset privacy principles and is possible today through the use of bank secrecy methods and resources.

2. Privacy principles and concepts to protect personal and business assets exist today, and choices are available to those who claim their freedom.

3. Preservation of personal and career information from data banks is essential to keeping privacy rights. Guard personal identifiers and financial data to protect business and personal financial information. Knowing personal privacy requirements and attitude are keys to obtaining and keeping financial privacy.

4. Dependence on government-sponsored programs and benefits may distort the judgment of those receiving benefits. Independence and objective thinking are crucial to maintaining privacy and freedom.

5. Conflicting material interests influence judgment and decisions, as individuals are motivated by security and money, at the expense of objective reasoning and rational thinking.

6. Privacy, particularly money and asset privacy, is essential to freedom. Without choices to keep private property private, one will not enjoy the security of having his/her life's business remain confidential. High-level financial privacy can be achieved today through utilizing resources conducive to keeping money and banking secrecy.

NOTES:

1. R. Morgan Griffin, "The Scary Truth about Medical Identity Theft," WebMD, February 2, 2007.

2. Kieran Nicholson, "Hundreds of Patients at Risk of ID Theft," DenverPost.com, December 7, 2007.

3. Unidentified reporter questions Bush on camer: Bush Admits That Iraq Had Nothing To Do With 911, Interview date unknown, posted on YouTube, August 23, 2006. http://www.youtube.com/watch?v=f_A77N5WKWM.

4. Vincent Bugliosi, *The Prosecution of George W. Bush For Murder* (New York, NY: Vanguard Press, 2008), 77.

5. Ibid., ix.

6. Dr. Steven E. Jones, "Why Indeed Did the WTC Buildings Completely Collapse?" *Journal of 911 Studies,* September 2006, vol. 3, http://www.Journalof911Studies.com.

7. Interview of Larry Silverstein, Leaseholder, World Trade Center, America Rebuilds: A Year at Ground Zero, PBS Documentary, 2002. See YouTube video at http://www.youtube.com/watch?v=7WYdAJQV100, posted August 28, 2006.

8. Grant Hall, *Privacy Crisis: Identity Theft Prevention Plan and Guide to Anonymous Living* (Las Vegas, NV: James Clark King, LLC, 2006), 375; www.PrivacyCrisis.com.

FOUR

Money Secrets

"Don't find fault, find a remedy."
—Henry Ford, Founder, Ford Motor Company

"OLD SCHOOL" BANKING SECRECY

Money belts loaded with hundred-dollar bills were strapped around his waist, chest, and ankles. Pressure against bare skin made him itch, but he kept focused.

Frankfurt had been uncomfortable, as he was sure the "suits" had singled him out and were ready to strip-search him, steal three-fourths of his life's savings, and deport him after a German-style kangaroo court—or worse. Was his paranoia kicking in again after a long hibernation? Or was his caution, verging on fear, justified? A little of both, he suspected.

Zurich was cultured, cool, and rainy—a welcome change of scenery; it even smelled clean.

Daydreams of five and a half years ago brought images of Swiss shopkeepers sweeping the sidewalks in front of their stores. Some of the more compulsive proprietors could be found on their hands and knees scrubbing the sidewalks in the wee morning hours. He remembered how they stayed open late, often until ten o'clock in the evenings.

He reminisced. Daydreaming helped relieve the stress. *Conscious meditation.*

The customs agent glanced at his U.S. passport and waved him through the gate without so much as a nod or a look in the eye. No "Welcome to Switzerland." Nothing. *Hard-ass Swiss.*

Alex Corbin felt relieved but did not relax until he had secured his suitcase, flagged a Mercedes taxi, and given the English-speaking driver the address. Once inside, he enjoyed the ride as the windy day and rain continued, making the October afternoon cooler than the Los Angeles weatherman had predicted.

The cabbie drove efficiently, swerving and passing slower cars, and he did not say a word through speedy freeway travel. He exited toward a discreet end of the business district. No tall skyscrapers—only modest shops and office buildings.

With one eye on the road and a second searching for the destination address, the driver carefully applied the brakes as he spotted the building. With the precision of a racecar driver making a pit stop, he jumped out to open the trunk that held Alex's lone suitcase, nodded his approval at the ten-dollar tip, and drove away.

The door had no name on it. That was not uncommon. Once inside, he was greeted by Birgit, Prinz's secretary. She was tall, blond, wore no wedding ring, and spoke without a trace of an accent. How do *they* master three or four languages so well?

Alex slouched into a comfortable leather sofa and watched her walk from the lobby down the hall. Her hips moved *without* her moving them. *Naturally.* Minutes later, she returned.

"He will see you now."

Though dressed in a conservative-cut navy business skirt, with a matching jacket, white blouse, black high heels, and a ladies' Rolex on her wrist, her shape was evident. *Natural. It fit.* To be sure, he glanced again peripherally.

Her perfume was unusual: creamy, lavender. She peered over her glasses as she spoke, much like an older lady, but she wasn't old, at least, not *that* old.

He wanted to stare but resisted.

Albert Prinz presented him with a business card that advertised his vice presidency with discretion. Instead of the full name of the bank, a four-letter, two-syllable acronym was on the card with a phone number. No address.

The banker explained the fiduciary account-opening procedures, shoved a stack of triplicate forms toward Alex, and inquired as to the nature of the deposit.

"Cash," Alex said.

Prinz glanced at the briefcase.

"Actually, I have it on me."

"Would you like me to leave you for a few moments so that you can get more comfortable?"

"Yes."

Swiss bankers loved the ever-weakening dollar President Reagan had committed to making even weaker for the sake of foreign trade. The conversion rate was 2.14 SF to 1 USD in 1983.

Five minutes later, Prinz returned, grabbed the stacks of bills, and left the room to count them. Meanwhile, Alex waited, gazing at ceiling corners, doorknobs, and the filing cabinet, searching for hidden cameras. And he wondered about Birget.

Prinz returned, claimed there was a hundred dollars less than the figure Alex had written on the paper, cocked his head, and waited. Alex knew better but said nothing. *The cost of doing business.*

It took another half hour to complete the paperwork. Prinz provided the account number and suggested he not forget it. Maybe he should tattoo it somewhere—never mind. His memory was photographic, at least for now.

The bank agreed to hold all statements indefinitely. They had a copy of his passport on file and a San Bernardino mail-drop address, compliments of Skip, the Vietnam vet with ulcers, half a right leg, and one kidney. Nothing else tied to his identity.

Swiss bankers promised banking secrecy to foreign customers. Tax evasion was not a crime in Switzerland, and if charges were ever brought against a foreigner who was suspected of holding unreported funds in a Swiss account, the case would have to be tried in Switzerland. It was all in the books he had read by those touting offshore investments, the gold bugs, and those predicting *the end of days.*

His friend had verified it all and vaguely explained his experiences on the matter, without encouragement. Prinz had explained as much, too.

He was not concerned about the Swiss bankers breaching secrecy contracts with their foreign customers. Switzerland, the premier banking haven of the day, had too much to lose, and bankers more to risk by opening their mouths than by keeping them shut. At least, that was the case today.

Prinz presented him with a metal cup with the bank's logo on it as they shook hands and parted. "For the fine California wines."

Alex faked a smile, shook hands, and left the conference room.

He nodded as Birget smiled when he passed her on his way out, thought briefly of inviting her for a drink after the bank closed, and decided against it.

THE HIGH PRICE OF PRIVACY

I met Billy Royal while attending an investment seminar at a Torrance, California, hotel during the1980s. His proprietary money flow indicators were in the beta-testing stage at the time, and he allowed me full use of his new software program.

Six feet three, muscular, fit, and appearing younger than his stated age of late 30s, Billy was a sophisticated Ivy League law school dropout who was determined to succeed as an entrepreneur.

We shared an interest in mega-vitamin and mineral therapy, and as we became well acquainted, he offered me use of his library. Later, as our relationship progressed, I had the honor of being his dinner guest on occasion, as he and his wife Elaine fed me until I was stuffed at weekend barbeques and evening parties.

One day he surprised me.

"Elaine's got a younger sister who is coming to visit for a month. We both like you, Grant. Want to drop by and meet Mary Sue next weekend?"

Being introduced by friends to a loved one has to rank as the highest of compliments, and I didn't grasp the full meaning of the gesture while in my 20s.

"Sure, I'd like that," I said.

Mary Sue and I hit it off and enjoyed a fabulous four weeks before she returned to Ohio to begin college. My not chasing her to Columbus may have been a huge mistake. We wrote, chatted by phone for a time, and lost track of each other.

Billy and I remained friends and talked mostly by telephone, as he began traveling periodically to Europe, where he purchased an interest in an Irish software company. Also, he and Elaine had twin baby boys.

Sometime later, I received a telephone message with a foreign number to call. The next day, I reached Billy at a Swiss hotel.

"Want to come to Geneva and be my guest for a couple of weeks?" he asked.

During my vacation three weeks later, I met him at the airport and had Swiss-style fun and the pleasure of a hands-on "educational vacation" in Geneva, compliments of one of my all-time most brilliant friends, Billy Royal.

He explained one evening that, after some years, he and Elaine were calling it quits. The marriage had become too much work. He needed to split his time between Europe and Los Angeles. She needed him at home. His boys needed a father. The business needed him, too. They argued. They no longer loved each other. The marriage could not be saved.

Financial obligations Billy faced included alimony and child support. Billy wanted to support his family, but Elaine wanted two or three times what it took to support herself and the children. California law may have been on her side. We'll never know. Billy Royal never returned to California.

He had long ago sold their Hollywood Hills property and replaced it with a larger, leased Sherman Oaks house. All business ties in California were severed.

He was liquid.

Armed with a dual citizenship from Ireland, by way of his business contribution, along with a huge income generated after many years of losses and struggle for market share, Billy and his Irish software company became a success. However, his marriage had failed.

During a workout in the morning of my last day as his guest, Billy surprised me once again.

"I sold it, Grant," he announced. "I spent everything I had, plus borrowed money, to make it go. It was time. I'm going to relax and travel." And he did.

During the 1970s and1980s, it was possible to utilize the banking secrecy laws offered by Switzerland and certain other first-world countries. Conditions favored the path to foreign investments, as the burden to report investment income, whether fiduciary or self-directed, was placed on the investor.

Disclosure of an American or other foreign account holder's name by a Swiss banker was a crime in Switzerland. Tax evasion was not.

The Austrian Sparbuch account was a bearer account opened with only an account numerical identifier, and the holder of the passbook could invest and make deposits without questions.

Liechtenstein foundations offered such bulletproof privacy protection that the Swiss reportedly used them instead of Swiss banks.

Today, the Sparbuch no longer exists, and Liechtenstein, following the Swiss' unraveling of bank secrecy, is not recommended as a safe haven for money.

Based on our conversations, I do not believe Billy Royal paid U.S. income taxes on the huge capital gains realized from the sale of his foreign software company. However, I am not sure.

Billy cashed out completely, stashed his money in banks in Switzerland, Austria, Liechtenstein, the Cayman Islands, and Belize. And he had a lot of it to stash. This, too, I learned on my last day with him in Geneva, but I did not want to know and never received the details of Billy Royal's foreign investments.

I did not know it was "goodbye" forever, when I left Switzerland as Billy's guest. He was a perfectionist and a businessman used to the price one sometimes pays for success. And he wasn't taking any unnecessary risks with people who might rat him out to whatever agencies or courts might want him—myself included.

Using his Irish passport, Billy skipped out and became invisible to the world: family, friends, former business associates, and any court or tax agency that may have wanted to know his whereabouts. Once he made the break, no one in his former life ever heard from him again.

Some years ago, I received a phone call from Elaine Royal, Billy's former wife. One of the twins had been killed in an accident. "Will you come to the funeral, Grant?" she sobbed.

Through tears while reliving the memories of a different era, Elaine, the twin brother of the now-deceased young man, and I shared reminiscences of days gone forever.

Billy Royal was not at his son's funeral. The price of high-level privacy is high indeed.

During the reception, a beautiful woman with auburn hair and features I immediately recognized approached me.

"I'm so glad you came," she said. Her two children and husband sat on the sofa across the room.

"Why did you stop writing and calling?" she wondered.

"Because I'm an idiot," I offered.

"I loved you," she whispered.

"I love you," I muttered.

FOREIGN BANKS BREACH BANK SECRECY AGREEMENTS

Banking secrecy is for the purpose of protecting your money from being discovered by anyone.

You may want to hide money from disgruntled exes, government agents, greedy lawyers, or other crooks after your hard-earned cash.

Though it had inherent risks, keeping your money a secret used to be simpler than it is today.

Can high-level financial privacy and banking secrecy *really* be achieved today? It can. However, bank secrecy is different today. Not necessarily more difficult than during the 1970s and 1980s—just different.

Swiss banking is not a private affair today, and though it is hard to believe, the Swiss have lost their reputation as the once-great bastion of banking secrecy. Consider the Union Bank of Switzerland (UBS) matter as a landmark case of selling out clients under pressure from the U.S. government.

> "In a separate matter, UBS has already transferred account data on several hundred clients, after admitting to aiding tax fraud through hidden offshore accounts. The bank agreed in February of last year to pay $780 million as part of a deal to avoid criminal prosecution for helping wealthy Americans evade taxes. A whistleblower in that case, Bradley Birkenfeld, began serving a 40-month prison sentence on January 8, 2010."[1]

Rather than take the word of Swiss bankers who are selling out their customers, do you think there may be a safer jurisdiction than the late great banking haven of Switzerland?

How about Liechtenstein, the tiny country where some of the most prudent Swiss are reputed to keep their money? Of all the countries on record as having bank secrecy to offer investors requiring discretion, those in the know would not have expected this small country to relinquish the secrecy of their account holders to foreign tax collectors, government agency men, and others. After reading the piece that follows, I have little confidence in most foreign bankers, wherever they may be and regardless of whatever bank secrecy laws may currently be in place.

> "The tiny principality, a financial center wedged between Switzerland and Austria, is seeking to be removed from a blacklist of tax havens and will now offer bilateral tax deals for cooperating in cases of tax fraud and tax evasion."[2]

When Switzerland and Liechtenstein bankers lose their guts and renege on their promises to keep customers' money safe and secret, others will surely follow, and it matters not what their constitution says in regard to bank secrecy or what laws may have protected account holders in the past.

That said, all is not lost. You can, with enough knowledge and the right resources, create your own banking secrecy while operating within the bounds of the legal system in your home jurisdiction. This means careful consideration of your privacy requirements and the selection of entities and resources as described in this book.

BANK SECRECY WITHOUT DEPENDENCE

He awakened to the smell of coffee, having overslept and missed his workout.

Travel-stimulated dreams? Airplane food? The ginko or phosphatidylserine formula? Maybe.

She brought his coffee and noticed his wandering mind.

"Dreams?"

"Yeah."

After breakfast and a shower, he was off.

That first Swiss "vacation," now twenty-five years ago, popped in and out of his consciousness all morning. And he had returned every few years. Prinz remained loyal, and Birget patched him through to Prinz's home phone as necessary when the eight-hour time difference was ignored or forgotten. Birget.

Driving toward the bank, Alex slipped on a wig and sunglasses and changed into the "costume" kept for such occasions. On went the black fedora, fake mustache, clip earrings, and red scarf. Never mind the plates. They were taken care of with the spray paint designed to block photo images.

The car registration. He smiled to himself.

The Limited Partnership ATM card issued by one of the big U.S. brokerage firms said, "Arthur Andrews Williams Limited," along with an expiration date. His name as signer was not on the card. However, it was buried deep within the broker's microfiche records.

They mailed a new card to the Channel Islands address every few years. Domestic brokers did not insist on sending the monthly statements monthly, now that he had opted to receive them online. He made certain there were no ties to him or the family in any paperwork going through the U.S. mail but only at the brokerage office, in case he ever needed to prove he legally controlled the account.

He withdrew $1,200, pulled out the receipt and card, and was off to purchase money orders for payment of a stack of bills. The amounts were committed to memory earlier that morning.

Some $1,100 and change, in the form of Western Union money orders purchased at two convenience stores, would satisfy the payments-due stack for a while.

The trust account was next. Time to raid Teton Grand Silver Spring Living Trust's money for household expenses, most of which would be settled with cash for food, gas, and other essentials. Other than that, more money orders would be used to mail a couple of payments. Later.

Once he returned to the house, he took refuge in the guest house-office. It was quiet, and the online work began.

His proxy server would not make it through the online brokerage account firewalls. So he never bothered. Logging in, he scrolled down the menu, noticed end-of-day closes for current positions, buy stops being hit, and one sell stop order "mental stop" within a hair of his loss limit. *Weakness begets weakness.* He entered a sell at the market for his pilot position, taken two days before. The other weak sister may go out the door tomorrow. *Be patient.* The charts told him three more buys were probable next week. *Get liquid. The first loss is usually the cheapest.*

Automatic pilot. No more tape watching. No emotion.

It was a bull market.

"BANKING" WITHOUT A BANK

Shirley Corbin completed the bookkeeping. Three checks payable to Strong Willow Bark Limited Liability Company, along with a stack of money orders and a few payments made in cash, had been gathered and entered as receipts from online sales prior to her beginning the trip to the check cashing store.

"Hello, Mrs. Corbin."

"Good morning, Irene."

Irene barked an order to the new associate in Spanish. Shirley understood the words "good customer" and smiled to herself.

After a quick swipe of the card and a check that their figures matched, she took the cash, said goodbye to Irene and her new part-time cohort, and was out the door.

She kept her hand on the concealed pistol, as she walked through the parking lot and glanced from side to side during the thirty-yard jaunt to the SUV. Once inside, she locked up, placed the Glock on the seat, and gave him a quick call.

"OK."

"I'm in the office. I'll meet you out front," Alex replied.

Together, they walked toward the concealed money safe in the attached garage. Under his sportcoat, he carried the AK with folding stalk and 100-round, circular clip. Inside the safe, he had placed a

.44 Magnum loaded with 240-grain hollow points. He opened it and checked the Magnum; they then made the "deposit" and went inside to balance the books for the household account and the LLC.

A SAFE "CURRENT ACCOUNT"

Later, during the afternoon, they traveled into the city and stopped at the branch of a community bank. They kept a safe deposit box in the name of the Nevada Family Limited Partnership at this branch. They had no other accounts here but held a household account in the name of their living trust at another branch of the same bank. This location had been requested to keep the partnership under the radar, as it was recorded nowhere else in the bank's database.

She called the clerk, who inserted the key along with Alex's, and the medium-sized safety deposit box was unlocked. Once inside, they shared the viewing room where bullion coins were added along with other cash equivalents.

Next, they drove to the other end of town, where their anonymous safe deposit box was kept in total secrecy. No names, IDs, Social Security Numbers, nothing. Only a private business facility of secure, bank-type vaults, without government regulations, where thousands of like-minded privacy seekers walked in, entered passwords, went through the scanner, and entered the back room, where they could be assured their secrets would be kept: secrets of valuables, gold, rare coins, jewelry, foreign currency, dollars, hoards of value of every type imaginable. Guns, too.

Once they were inside the private viewing room, Alex opened their box, and Shirley checked notes and inventoried the contents.

Two foreign currencies and dollars were deposited, along with documents and gold coins. She took out a necklace. His gift.

As they left the vault, passwords were again entered and accepted by the proprietary software system.

They passed through the steel door, waved to Mr. Wood, the proprietor, and walked toward their parked vehicle three blocks away, planning where to go for dinner.

NEW ERA "FUGITIVE LEVEL" BANKING SECRECY (WITH RISKS)

Jane Collins e-mailed me, requesting I call her back on her direct number at a pre-designated time. I did. She agreed to let me reproduce our interview, which I have included for educational and informational purposes only. I do NOT advise anyone to attempt duplicating Jane's money privacy methods as she related them to me during this interview.

Always follow the laws in your given jurisdiction, and DO NOT give a fake identification or other false information to financial institutions. Those who provide falsified documents to a foreign or domestic bank may risk losing their money and be subject to civil or criminal charges.

The interview follows:

Jane: "Grant, I read your book, *Privacy Crisis*, and wanted to thank you for it."

Grant: "Tell me about your experiences of living the privacy lifestyle."

Jane: "I have been using high-level privacy techniques and methods for a number of years. Very high-level privacy and secrecy of my money is necessary."

Grant: "Why did you start living under the radar?"

Jane: "My divorce and being stalked and abused by my ex-husband."

Grant: "I'm sure it was difficult."

Jane: "I made the decision to walk away from it and never see my relatives or old friends again."

Grant: "I see."

Jane: "I refused to become a victim and to depend on the ineffective legal system. Most books I read prior to yours had outdated, irrelevant information on keeping money a secret. This was a priority for me, as he had previously used investigators to track my bank accounts and my job."

Grant: "How were you able to lose your abusive, stalker ex-husband?"

Jane: "I read and studied your book. I'm known as someone else. I rent under my alternate identity, instructed the credit bureaus to freeze my credit files, and my car is held by a trust. My employer sends checks to a company formed for my privacy. I have made it my business to learn how to protect my privacy. I'm certain he will never find me."

Grant: "You sound confident, Jane."

Jane: "I became someone else, completely. I receive payments for my work as a technical person in the hospital industry through an LLC. I cash checks and store the cash, gold, and foreign currency in a safe deposit box that cannot be traced to me. Also, I use a home safe. I'm mobile. I can move on a few hours notice. I have worked in three states in the last six years."

Grant: "I'm sure you're under stress with the pressures associated with frequent moves and worrying about being discovered."

Jane: "Yeah. But, the pressure is a trade-off for avoiding further injuries and possible death. The last time he beat me, he told me if I ever took off again without telling him where I was, he'd kill me. I'm a thinker. I did not make this decision off the cuff, so to speak. I weighed the pros and cons and elected to do it this way. Basically, I shut off my emotions completely. I had to, in order to be successful. The life I'm leading now is better, much better, than letting that son of a bitch continue to beat me."

Grant: "How do you bank in total secrecy?"

Jane: "I expect most of what used to work doesn't anymore. Foreign bank accounts are a joke for the average American. Unless you don't need the money, a foreign bank account is a bad idea, today. The UBS case illustrates the powers of Big Brother—even over the once-sacred Swiss banking secrecy laws. Today, my way—the changing of an identity completely— is the only way to avoid discovery."

Grant: "Explain that, Jane."

Jane: "I use the banks that are easy to deal with. I follow the illegal aliens and copy their methods of money secrecy. Debit cards that double as a bank account have worked. It's a matter of using identification that's acceptable to them, having the guts to pull it off, and assuming the risk of losing what money is on deposit if I'm discovered. I take those chances."

Grant: "Yes."

Jane: "A number of check-cashing services and loan centers offer debit cards that double as a bank account without the ability to write checks. I have used a couple of these debit cards. I needed a valid identification to get started. These institutions are the new "banks" for those who want privacy. The way I see it, it's my money, and if I have to use a different name, that's my business, not someone else's.

Generally, several forms of identification are acceptable. These are a state-issued driver's license, photo identification issued from a state government, a domestic or foreign passport, a foreign driver's license, an alien ID, or a military ID. And usually they want to see some sort of other identification, such as a credit card, an insurance card, or school identification.

Suffice it to say that I jumped through the identification hoops successfully. I'm not going to say what I used, but it worked. I was scared to death at first, but I'm not anymore. Like I said, I need a bank account, so I assume the risk of having it discovered that I used a new name to open it, and I could lose all my money on deposit."

Grant: "Yes. I understand that financial institutions periodically audit their accounts and sometimes make discoveries that lead them to ask a lot of questions. That can result in their freezing the funds of a customer until he or she proves they are on the up and up."

Jane: "Yeah, they do. Actually, that happened to me once. They froze my account, and I lost a couple hundred dollars. I just let it go. The key is to keep the account balance relatively low, so that if they attempt to steal it, your loss is small."

Grant: "I see."

Jane: "With a debit card that is reloadable, I have to have a mailing address to receive the card. The card is good for three or four years before it expires. I can load cash onto it, withdraw cash from ATMs, use it for debit card purchases, make online purchases, and receive online deposits for things I sell online—the works. I can even have my checks received from my work deposited into the account if I want to. The key is to keep the account balance low, which I do. I go to the ATM machine often and withdraw cash and store it either in my home safe or in my offsite safe deposit box that has no record of my name associated with it. The best part is that I can see all of the account activity online, and there are no bank statements—only the account history available to me online through a password. The obvious downside is the relatively high fees associated with maintaining the account and the risk of losing the account because some auditor wants to reverify identification or something."

Grant: "It sounds as if the method you are using allows for your money privacy. Do you have any recommendations as far as which debit cards to use for a bank account?"

Jane: "No. There are a number of these. Go to most of the loan centers and check-cashing services that cash checks and provide other services. They don't ask too many questions, though they all ask enough. These companies sell the cards to customers. They are issued by several different banks. Check-cashing stores in the U.S., Canada, and parts of Europe have them."

Grant: "Anything else?"

Jane: "Yes. Within the last few months, I opened a business bank account under the name of a Limited Liability Company. The LLC is a registered Nevada company. The manager of record is a trust established for the sole purpose of being the company manager. A nominee signs the Nevada Secretary of State form, and she is actually the administrative trustee of the trust. This makes me, as the company manager, anonymous."

Editor's Note: See Trust Manager Principle in *Privacy Crisis: Identity Theft Prevention Plan and Guide to Anonymous Living,* by Grant Hall, at www.PrivacyCrisis.com.

Grant: "Tell me about the new bank account."

Jane: "I formed the LLC under the same name I use as my alternate name. The checks I receive from work are payable to the LLC, the same name as my alternate name, with 'LLC' included. Sometimes I receive checks payable to me under my alternate name only. The checks go through the bank-clearing process fine, whether they are payable to my alternate name or to the company with 'LLC' included.

"Also, the LLC bank account is entirely on the up and up. That is, the bank has my real identification. I have the company registered anonymously, as you recommend in *Privacy Crisis.* I elected to open this account after some years, and I believe it is safe from his discovery.

"The bank is in a tiny town with only one branch. The statements have the LLC's name *only*, and my name as the signer on the account is only on the bank's internal records. A credit check was not completed on me when I opened the account. I expect the account would not come up in a search done by a private investigator. The account is in a state far away from my previous home or job, my name is not on the account as the account holder but only as a signer, and it is hidden from view when accounts are pulled up under account holders at the bank."

Grant: "I see."

Jane: "And the LLC Articles of Organization, a public record, only have the organizer's name on them, not mine. He cannot find me through the Nevada LLC."

Grant: "Sounds like you have done a lot to preserve your money privacy. Jane, I appreciate the time you were able to spend with me and your willingness to share the information and your experiences."

Jane's case of using the check-cashing store, combined with anonymous safe deposit boxes, while "banking" under an alternate name, is an example of total banking secrecy. However, her risk is being found out by the check-cashing store where she cashes her checks. And, as she stated, she has already suffered one loss, albeit a modest one, when the bank holding the debit card attempted to verify her information. During this inquiry, Jane elected to walk away from this account while taking her loss.

Her second type of bank secrecy utilizes a small community bank combined with an anonymously registered company and has worked for her as well.

The risks are high, and the potential for losses is great for those who attempt to adopt a fugitive level of banking secrecy, as Jane has experienced. In her case, it was worth the risk, as the potential harm from being discovered by her abuser motivated her to go to extreme measures to make her money anonymous.

MODERN MONEY PRIVACY ISSUES

Today, the Corbin family and others practice banking secrecy in the U.S., while utilizing available resources and privacy tactics necessary to keep their business and investments secure from potential privacy invasions. While many privacy tactics unrelated to the subject of bank secrecy are necessary to secure one's life and provide a foundation on which to build financial privacy, the principles and concepts I have used for privacy are beyond the scope of this book. They are, however, fully explained in my first book, *Privacy Crisis: Identity Theft Prevention Plan and Guide to Anonymous Living*, available at www.Privacy-Crisis.com.

It should be noted that the freedom to keep one's money private is a basic right to privacy, but somewhere along the way, governments, both in the U.S. and abroad, began to believe they had the right to track and trace their citizens' store of value—that is, their hard-earned "stored labor"—in order to make certain that dissatisfied citizens would not abandon ship and stop supporting the giant debt machine behind these governments. You must understand, valued reader, that human collateral is all that currently backs the once-great United States dollar, now a sinking ship in the world currency markets. Controllers of government "representatives" managed to scare these so-called representatives into voting for discretionary bailouts rather than let free market forces determine the outcomes of mismanaged businesses.

These bailouts and the necessary money creation from debt to execute them diluted the currency so severely that the debt is now impossible to pay *unless* the currency is further devalued, which will result in more and more losses of your purchasing power over the years to come. Can you say *Brazil*?

While considering the reasons for government tracking citizens' money, it becomes clear why it is necessary to have financial privacy as a means of assuring your continued freedom. For without knowledge of what you own and where it is located, even the most clever thieves, whether government agents or street thugs, will not have a clue how to seize property belonging to a business or individual threatening to upset their apple cart of propaganda. And make no mistake about it: protestors, writers, and freedom fighters are often targeted and singled out for harassment or worse.

While it is possible today to shield your money entirely from anyone legally, government included, through the use of anonymous safe deposit boxes, home safes, and separate entities that you do not own but still control, there is a trend for the current fascists who control your government to seize property first when they want to do it, in order to "break" a particular subject, take possession of said money and/or property, and make the abused citizen prove them wrong in court. This is a long-term, expensive affair at best, without promise of a favorable outcome.

By far the best asset seizure prevention plan is high-level secrecy, combined with a sound entity-holding structure when substantial assets are at risk. The use of anonymously registered entities will be discussed in future chapters, as well as their application for holding certain property and businesses.

For the individual or family wishing to avoid having their bank accounts seized, the use of check-cashing services may be appropriate, as these pseudo-banking operations can be used to cash business or personal checks, while allowing the business manager or employee to take immediate possession of their money—without holds placed on checks and without the risk of a bank account seizure to satisfy an alleged or true payment obligation. Some sophisticated privacy advocates, both foreign and domestic, have discovered the privacy and near risk-free uses of check-cashing stores, the subject of the next chapter.

SUMMARY

1. Banking secrecy was provided to account holders by many offshore banks prior to and during the 1970s and 1980s. Certain types of accounts have been discontinued, and some traditional banking havens' secrecy laws, Switzerland and Liechtenstein, for example, have been compromised.

2. It may be beneficial for certain individuals and companies to utilize the services of foreign banks for privacy and protection of assets today. The advice of a competent attorney is recommended for asset protection planning. Readers are advised by the author to follow all applicable laws in their given jurisdiction.

3. Certain privacy advocates create secret bank accounts through the use of online bank accounts, debit cards, company accounts, and the utilizing of private safe deposit boxes. Fake identification has been used as a means for "fugitive level banking"—a practice that enables the account holder to operate without any ties whatsoever to his or her old identity. Bank auditors review accounts on a regular basis and freeze questionable bank accounts until the account-holder answers identity-related or other security questions.

4. Banking privacy, and privacy in general, is more expensive than maintaining traditional banking and a traditional lifestyle, from both an emotional and financial standpoint.

5. Certain families, individuals, and businesses place a high value on their financial privacy and establish banking secrecy through the use of check-cashing stores, anonymous safe deposit boxes, safes, and privately registered, separate legal entities.

6. The author does not recommend breaking laws in any jurisdiction for banking privacy.

NOTES:

1. "Swiss Government Bows to Court Ruling: Will Review UBS Tax Agreement,"
    Accounting Web, January 28, 2010, http://www.accountingweb.com/topic/
    tax/swiss-government-bows-court-ruling-will-review-ubs-tax-agreement.

2. "Liechtenstein eases bank secrecy amid tax crackdown," elEconomista.
    es, December 3, 2009, http://www.eleconomista.es/empresas-finanzas/
    noticias/1094855/03/09/Liechtenstein-eases-bank-secrecy-amid-tax-
    crackdown.html.

♦ FIVE ♦

Check-Cashing Stores

"The question isn't who is going to let me; it's who is going to stop me."
—Ayn Rand, Novelist

THE NEW "BANKS"

Some years ago, only "undesirable" banking customers utilized these third cousins to the commercial banks. Now, as money and banking privacy erodes and is taken from the average Joe or Jane—(not you, valuable reader), and safety of currency becomes a top priority, both individuals and businesses are turning to these operations for the immediate clearance of their checks and for taking possession of their cash the day their check is presented for payment.

Often the amounts charged to cash checks appear expensive on the surface to the novice privacy seeker or prudent businessperson who wants to contain costs and maintain full control over the end result of his business receipts: cash.

I have found these businesses to offer a fair charge for their check-cashing services, as compared to commercial banks. As of this writing, business checks and payroll checks may be converted into cash at many of these establishments at a rate of about 1.9 percent to 2.9 percent, depending on your location. While this may seem excessive, consider checking account bank fees and additional business banking fees for a business account that will often exceed $75 to $125 per month.

How about using an offshore bank for business purposes? Offshore banking is particularly expensive for individual account holders and those requiring business accounts, especially when merchant account services are needed. Base fees for an offshore merchant account often exceed $200 per month, and this amount is only for maintaining the account. In addition, a substantial amount is normally kept as collateral for charge-backs and security by a foreign bank that has a merchant account tied to it.

Foreign banks often take thirty days or more to clear checks drawn on a U.S. bank.

The management of a business account that holds investments by offshore institutions through fiduciary accounts or self-directed investments will be more expensive, for Americans, than in domestic institutions. Services in Switzerland will be superior to domestic banks, but you can no longer bank secretly there if you are not a Swiss citizen, based on my analysis of Swiss banking trends.

Domestic check-cashing stores offer value to the account holder on several levels: immediate clearance of checks and ability to take the possession of cash when the check is cashed, no stored money with the financial institution, and less privacy-invasive information requirements for opening the account.

The real and hidden value of using a check-cashing establishment as your "bank" is the total control one maintains over the cash generated for payment of goods and services, subcontracting, or employment. No longer will a business or an individual have to fear the freezing and/or seizure of a personal or business bank account. Once you cash your checks, business or personal, simply carry your cash away, store it in your designated spot for safe-keeping (see chapter 6 on Safes and Safe Deposit Boxes), and go on your joyful way without leaving a trace as to the whereabouts of your cash.

Full and complete banking secrecy and total control of money is offered to those with the resources and power to take responsibility to create it, in the U.S. or abroad, through the use of foreign and domestic check-cashing services.

I have used check-cashing establishments for a number of years and have never given my home address, Social Security Number, Employer Identification Number, driver's license, or a home telephone number, prior to cashing a check. I have cashed business and personal checks with multiple companies at a number of locations.

Generally, one can provide a copy of his or her passport, a mail-drop address, proof of business registration (Secretary of State documentation found on the website), a copy of the Articles of Organization (p record, Limited Liability Company), and proof of control over the company, for checks presented for payment, by providing a copy of certain pages of the trust designated as manager of the business. (See *Trust Manager Principle,* as explained in *Privacy Crisis: Identity Theft Prevention Plan and Guide to Anonymous Living.*)

Based on my experiences and those of others who have used my methods to obtain financial privacy, it is obvious that the use of check-cashing stores is far more private and poses less risk to the business manager or individual who chooses to create his/her own "current account" for cash withdrawals, as needed, and without the risk of having their funds seized by anyone or any agency for any reason.

I expect the managers of the Liberty Dollar makers, the NORFED Corporation, wish they had opted for a banking secrecy plan to prevent the seizure of their bank account that occurred in 2007, when FBI agents raided their offices and seized their property and money.[1]

For managers and families to plan ahead, prepare for the worst, and take the steps necessary to keep money and property from being seized is prudent, even though these measures will be more expensive than traditional banking. Astute business managers and household heads view the extra expenses allocated to a high-level financial privacy plan as a necessary cost of doing business and build these costs into their business plans and budgets.

It takes only one bank account seizure to put a family on the street or bankrupt a business. Banking secrecy and asset privacy is a worthwhile "insurance policy" and a hedge against a catastrophic event.

A huge advantage of using check-cashing services for converting your business or personal checks into cash lies in the breaking of the paper trail from the check itself to you. The buck (pun intended) stops at the point of cash issuance—from the check being deposited into the business account of the check-cashing service and the equivalent cash into your noble hands.

Once you have the cash in hand, you are free to spend it as you please, or invest the cash into whatever asset you deem necessary at the time, whether that be as a cash or money order deposit into an investment account of an entity that holds investment funds under your control, a privately held safe deposit box or safe, precious metals purchases, the buying of foreign currency, purchases of real property, collectibles, or goods and services.

It matters not what the funds are used for; you have "clean cash" without a full accounting link to you—a better privacy advantage than when you make withdrawals from a bank account held under your name, write checks for "cash," or use checks for purchasing investments or essential goods and services.

Part-time clerks employed at the check-cashing service businesses are the rule of the day, and they love to "rule over you" whenever possible. Typically, they do not know the meaning of an LLC and have never seen a trust. Their "script" comes with the questions that follow in a mock interview that is, based on my experiences, similar to what you will encounter as you begin to do business with the "banks" of choice for the privacy seeker, both in the U.S. and abroad.

Your answers should mirror those contained in the following simulated exchange, if you want to achieve my level of privacy.

SIMULATED INTERVIEW: CHECK-CASHING STORE ACCOUNT

The content of the following paraphrased interview is accurate as a description of my actual account-opening experiences with stores that cash business and personal checks. In all cases, either less information or exactly what is mentioned herein was required. In one case, no ID at all was needed. However, I had done business with the store prior to using their check-cashing services. It does indeed matter who you are when you develop your privacy lifestyle. Name changes have been made in this interview.

Clerk: "Hello. May I help you?"

Grant: "Hello. I manage a company and would like to cash checks payable to the business at your store."

Clerk: "Do you own the business?"

Grant: "I manage the business and have full control over the money received and the authority to cash the checks."

Clerk: "Who owns the business?"

Grant: "May I have the regional manager's name and telephone number? I would like to schedule an appointment to provide proper business documentation for the purpose of using your check-cashing services."

Clerk: "Wait here. I'll call my supervisor."

Grant: "OK."

Supervisor: "Do you own the business?"

Grant: "I manage the business and have full control of the business receipts."

Supervisor: "We need proof that you are authorized to cash checks for the business."

Grant: "OK. I can provide that proof. Are you the person who makes the decision to cash the business checks, once I provide proof that I have the authority to cash these checks?"

Supervisor: "I will have to call the area manager for his approval, once you provide proof to me."

Grant: "OK. I would like to meet with the area manager by appointment and provide the business documents at that time rather than leave these copies with you, as I do not want internal, confidential information on file unless I have an account with your company."

Supervisor: "He just walked in. I'll ask him if he can see you."

Area Manager: "Hello. I am Milton Maxhiltopper."

Grant: "Hello."

Area Manager: "Do you own the company for checks you want to cash with us?"

Grant: "I am the manager of the Limited Liability Company and have full control and the authority to cash checks made payable to the LLC."

Area Manager: "We need proof that you have this authority."

Grant: "Here is the copy of the title page and signature page of the Palm Blue Rainbow Irrevocable Trust, of which I am the trustee. This is the copy of the Willow Spot, LLC company registration obtained from the Nevada Secretary of State website today that lists Palm Blue Rainbow Irrevocable Trust as the manager of Willow Spot, LLC."

Area Manager: "We need a copy of the business license."

Grant: "This is an Internet business, and there are no license requirements except the business license equivalent that is paid to the Nevada Secretary of State at the time the company is registered, when such a payment is required. As you can see from the registration of the company, the 'business license' is current."

Area Manager: "We need a copy of the Articles of Organization."

Grant: "OK. This is a copy of the two-page Articles of Organization for Willow Spot, LLC that is a public record. As you can see, the organizer of the company and my attorney, Mr. Crommzinny, is also the resident agent of record."

Area Manager: "May we call him?"

Grant: "Of course."

Ten minutes later the Area Manager returns. I had taken a seat across the room and return to speak to him through the plate glass window.

Area Manager: "Your attorney verified the information you provided."

Grant: "Thank you for calling him."

Area Manager: "We need your driver's license."

Grant: "I use my passport as my proof of identity."

Area Manager: "May I see it?"

Grant: "Yes."

Area Manager copies it and returns to the window.

Area Manager: "We need your Social Security Number, home address, home telephone number, and thumbprint."

Grant: "Here are the addresses for the business and my personal mail. Since I do not use a home phone, I can provide you with my office number."

The area manager goes to a computer to verify that the addresses given to him are real street addresses.

Area Manager: "What's your social?"

Grant: "I don't have it."

Area Manager: "Normally, we like to have a Social Security Number on file, but we do not always have this requirement, as certain customers who use our service do not have Social Security Numbers."

Grant: *"You mean like all the illegal-alien Mexicans and others who skip the tax system," I think, ponder whether to say it or not, and don't.*

Area Manager: "We sometimes ask for a thumbprint prior to cashing checks."

Grant: "Mr. Maxhiltopper, with all due respect for your caution and due diligence prior to cashing checks issued to Willow Spot, LLC, I do not provide fingerprints for banking services and would like to request a substitute identification method."

Area Manager: "That won't be necessary. Where will the checks payable to the business come from?"

Minutes later, I am issued a banking card that contains information on the magnetic strip.

My cell telephone number was verified, as they called me on it while in the store.

One check was cashed today, and more will follow, once they are received.

They have a copy of my passport, the title page and signature page of the trust that manages the LLC, the LLC Articles of Organization (a two-page public document without my name on it), a copy of the

Willow Spot, LLC Secretary of State company registration (another public record piece of information available to anyone with an Internet connection), a business and personal mailing address, and a cell telephone number I plan to replace.

Do they know who is behind the business of Willow Spot, LLC? Yes. I want it that way, because I want a legal claim to money generated by the business.

Can they call me at home, barge into my office, knock on my front door at home, locate my automobile through the Department of Motor Vehicles, or find me through a driver's license database? No.

I gave my word to the area manager that all checks payable to the business are guaranteed. They provide a valuable service, and I want to establish a business relationship that will last long term.

Essentially, I am invisible to the check-cashing service business, except when I appear to exchange company checks for cash. And the checks presented as payable to Willow Spot, LLC are endorsed with my illegible signature on the back of each check—above the check-cashing store's bank account information. These checks are deposited into and clear through the check-cashing store's company account. This is the information stored in databases and available to those who monitor negotiable instruments. Only the store has my limited personal information in their files.

Of course, my account balance is always at a zero balance, eliminating the possibility of any monetary confiscation, for any reason whatsoever, by anyone.

The above interview is an accurate account of what has occurred as I have opened accounts with a number of these companies over a period of years.

The bank secrecy provided to me in this exchange is more private than was banking with a Swiss bank thirty years ago, as per my experience. The only difference is that the foreign bank was offshore and was believed to offer bulletproof bank secrecy—a contract that appears to have been broken by certain Swiss banks two to three decades later. So what good does it do you to go through the hoop-jumping process of providing references to a Swiss bank or other foreign bank that claims to offer banking secrecy, if they change the rules in the middle of the deal?

The advantage of using a check-cashing store over a foreign bank account is that the check-cashing store will provide you with immediate credit for your "deposit," while requiring less personal and business information, than the foreign banks which once claimed to offer bank secrecy or that still claim to offer it today.

The disadvantage of using a check-cashing store rather than a foreign bank claiming to have bank secrecy for customers is that you have to lug the cash out of the store and find a safe place to put it. The solutions to these problems will be discussed at length in future chapters; the methods offered are based on my experiences in real time while under fire and are applicable and doable, whether you are living from paycheck to paycheck or have investment assets that need to be kept secret and free from seizure.

"BANK" WITHOUT A COMMERCIAL BANK: RELOADABLE DEBIT CARDS

The check-cashing service establishments and a few other businesses issue reloadable debit cards that function as a regular debit card and have features similar to a commercial bank account, while offering more privacy and convenience.

The reason many who live beneath the radar gravitate toward these types of accounts is because the institutions that issue them do not usually have requirements as stringent as the brick and mortar commercial banks—even though the institutions behind these reloadable debit cards are in fact banks. Also, the bank account/debit card account is normally not discovered in asset searches for several reasons: It is considered a debit card issued by a financial services company, not a bank. However, the account has a Federal Deposit Insurance Corporation (FDIC) policy attached to it, so in theory, at least, the account is a *real* bank account. But a private investigator or other asset searcher would be hard-pressed and would necessarily expend large amounts of time, effort, and money to locate such a bank account.

Why? During my extensive research on this subject, I discovered the process of debit card issuance, account service administration, and financial account recording by the bank to go like this: First, the check-cashing company or check-cashing store is the agent for the financial services company that issues the card. Account holder information is verified by the financial services company, and the card is mailed to the customer. A bank's name, the *sponsor*, will be on the card itself, and the account will be FDIC insured.

Are the funds actually held at the bank itself in the individual's name on the card? Yes and no. While the bank stands behind the accounts with their FDIC insurance policy as a safety net in case of insolvency, the actual account is not in the same database as checking and savings accounts opened by customers who walk in and open an account with the bank—when such services are available, that is. Therefore, since the bank standing behind the issuer of the debit card does not have an account on their books of the debit card account holder, the individual may in fact be able to practice a high level of bank privacy with this type of bank account.

Also, it is common for the sponsor bank to be in another state far away from where the card was purchased by the customer at the check-cashing store. Essentially, the financial privacy-seeking customer has two built-in advantages to using a debit card as a bank account, in addition to the aforementioned "cash and carry" advantage and the furnishing of less privacy-invasive personal and business information than required by a commercial bank—distance of the sponsoring bank and the non-traditional nature of the account itself.

Normally, an applicant for a reloadable debit card provides an identification and Social Security Number to the check-cashing store, which issues a temporary card for a nominal fee. The financial services company that manages the account verifies the information and mails the official card to the applicant's address within a week or two.

U.S. citizens are asked but not always required to provide a Social Security Number, which is later verified. Government identification, an address, and a telephone number are required.

Those with a foreign passport or an accepted form of foreign identification by the company issuing the card may also open an account, and of course, non-U.S. customers will not have an SSN to provide but must have a U.S. address in place, at least long enough to receive the card every few years. All account data is managed online or by telephone.

Essentially, the key features that make the reloadable debit cards a usable alternative to a traditional bank account are full usage of the account for direct deposits from one's employment; use as a debit card for purchases wherever Visa or MasterCard are accepted; the full use of automatic teller machines for cash withdrawals, both from domestic and foreign machines; receiving deposits for online payments when online vendors require a bank account for the deposit of funds; and cash deposits at the check-cashing store or through an agent such as Western Union.

Generally, there is a daily limit on deposits, an aggregate limit on the card of usually $10,000, and a daily ATM withdrawal limit.

The players that issue these cards come and go, and some merge with other companies. So the names behind the debit cards change from time to time. Metabank is the bank that sponsors the financial services company Netspend, now a Capital One company, and Check City and other check-cashing stores sell debit cards to customers serviced and issued by these institutions.

One can buy a reloadable card at a store that issues these cards, complete a short application form, and receive the card by mail within days, in most cases. A valid mailing address and certain identification requirements must be met. Some applicants have made substitutions for Social Security Numbers. For instance, some companies have accepted other identifiers, such as the number on a foreign passport or other number, instead of a Social Security Number. This has to be the case, as many of the reloadable debit card industry's customers are working illegally in the country and do not have Social Security Numbers.

In certain cases, a copy of a foreign identification or foreign passport has to be mailed to the financial services company issuing the card prior to the card being activated.

Identification requirements vary, as do other personal information data requirements. A state-issued driver's license, a state-issued identification card, an alien ID, a military ID, and a foreign or domestic passport have all been used to meet the identification requirements.

I have never heard of any ChexSystems requirements or credit checks as a requirement for opening an account, as is the case with certain commercial banks. Indeed, some of these companies advertise that "no one is turned down," but of course, this is not the case, as account opening requirements—though not as strict as commercial banks—have to be met.

The reloadable debit cards are for individuals, though some have been issued in company names. In some cases individuals and business managers have requested their company name be placed on the card, along with their first initial and last name, and these requests have been met. These efforts have been coordinated with the check-cashing store manager and the issuing company.

CHECK-CASHING RESOURCES

The following businesses have been accepting of company checks, as well as drafts and checks payable to individuals. As always, it matters a great deal *who you are,* as well as *what you know,* when you seek privacy services. A review of the behavior section of *Privacy Crisis: Identity Theft Prevention Plan and Guide to Anonymous Living* is recommended.

Checksmart
7001 Post Road
Dublin, OH 43016
Telephone: (800) 837-0381
www.checksmart.com

Checksmart has 252 stores in eleven states. Currently, the company has stores located in Arizona, California, Florida, Indiana, Kansas, Kentucky, Michigan, Missouri, Ohio, Utah, and Virginia. A number of the stores are open seven days a week, and some locations are open twenty-four hours each day.

Checks payable to a business or an individual may be cashed at competitive rates for this industry. The amount deducted for the check-cashing service is approximately 1.9 percent.

The stores have reciprocal agreements, a worthwhile convenience and a time-saver for those who may travel and need to use stores in different locations.

Through their relationship with financial services company, Insight, LLC, Checksmart sells the Insight prepaid MasterCard. This account is managed as an online bank account, and account numbers and routing numbers are provided to customers.

While check-writing services are not included with the account, money orders can be purchased online or at stores to pay bills.

The bank that provides the FDIC insurance to account holders is Urban Trust Bank.

Contact information:
Insight, LLC
600 Beacon Parkway West, Suite 901
Birmingham, AL 35209
Telephone: (877) 344-6744
www.insightcards.com
Urban Trust Bank
400 Colonial Center Parkway, Suite 150
Lake Mary, FL 32746
Telephone: (877) 344-6744
www.urbantrustbank.com

Legislation in some states has placed restrictions on the lending practices of check-cashing services, causing many to have revenue reductions, resulting in store closures. This information is according to my discussion with a manager in this industry.

Managers scramble for new business to take up the slack caused by revenue losses from money loans at high annual percentage rates. The result is that certain check-cashing services offer outstanding customer service to businesses and individuals.

Checksmart is one company that receives high marks for customer service, particularly in the West, where privacy-conscious business managers have been able to open an Insight prepaid MasterCard in the name of the business *without* providing an Employer Identification Number or a Social Security Number for the account. Individuals routinely open this same account under their names without Social Security Numbers, according to a management contact.

Holding an account in one's name or in the name of a company under one's control, without an Employer Identification Number or a Social Security Number, affords a bank secrecy advantage. These accounts will remain invisible *when* these identifiers are used during asset searches designed to provide information for a bank account garnishment. As per a management contact, these accounts will not surface during asset searches of bank accounts, as these customer accounts are buried within a corporate account and are segregated as individual accounts that are managed completely online—without a messy paper trail of bank account statements, cancelled checks, or bank wire transfer records.

The Insight prepaid MasterCard offers Automatic Clearing House services. ACH deposits, ACH debits, and cash may be deposited into the account. Automatic teller machines provide customers with cash withdrawal capability worldwide. Other available services include overdraft protection, real-time text alerts of account activity, free direct deposit, online bill payment services, and full-time support. The Insight prepaid debit card functions almost entirely like an online bank account.

Keep in mind that checks cashed by a check-cashing store reference the company account as the bank account used to clear the check.

Business managers with bank secrecy as a priority have used anonymous business registration principles to shield their identity from registered businesses. Checks cashed under a business name by a manager who cannot be identified on the Secretary of State registration empower this manager with financial privacy.

Privacy-conscious individuals have used multiple check-cashing services to enhance their personal privacy. For instance, a prepaid debit card has been purchased from one company, and this online account has been opened and used as an online bank account. A separate check-cashing service has been used to cash personal checks.

American Cash Express (ACE)
Corporate Headquarters:
American Cash Express
1231 Greenway Drive, Suite 600
Irving, TX 75038
Telephone: (972) 223-2274
Website: www.americancashexpress.com
E-mail: acepresident@acecashexpress.com

ACE had stores located in thirty-eight states as of this writing. Find one in your area through the website or through the corporate office.

The stores cash checks payable to businesses and individuals, at competitive rates.

While some extraordinary service has been provided by certain store managers, including cashing checks from a distance, followed by the wiring of funds to the payee by the store manager via MoneyGram, it must be recognized that store personnel do not stay in one place for long periods of time, and long-term relationships are difficult to establish due to these employment changes. It matters a great deal who you deal with at ACE if you want exceptional service to meet your individual needs, due to the differences in personnel experience and variances in the flexibility of each manager. However, you will find this to be the case with all check-cashing establishments and banks, as well.

Once a relationship has been established with a check-cashing service store manager, the astute, privacy-conscious individual or business manager can receive many of the same conveniences that are obtained from commercial banks but without the risks of having a bank account seized by government agencies, the tax man, or other criminals who have targeted your money.

Seizures of money from an account, wrongly or just, simply will not happen, when one keeps cash under his or her control. For instance, one business manager travels a great deal while attending to the management of a Limited Liability Company. His receipts come from a third-party credit card processor in the form of checks. In addition, money orders from retail customer orders and cash are received by mail. Once the checks and money orders are received, often by mail being forwarded, this traveling manager phones the check-cashing store manager and alerts him of the forthcoming receipts by priority mail delivery. Once the checks are received, the manager of the check-cashing store stamps them, deposits them into the store's company account, deducts the appropriate fees, and sends the funds by Money-Gram to the business manager. The business manager receives the confirmation number from the check-cashing store by telephone, goes to one of the many businesses that process MoneyGram transactions, and picks up his money.

All of these banking features have been obtained from check-cashing stores, when one has built the rapport necessary to do business at a distance with a manager.

In some cases too, the business manager has forwarded his company checks by ground carrier or priority mail to the check-cashing store and advises the check-cashing store manager to cash the checks and deposit the funds onto the debit card account issued by the check-cashing store. The funds are then immediately available for withdrawal by the traveling business manager, through one of many automatic teller machines (ATMs) available for use throughout the world. Though this is a rare service offered by a check-cashing store and would necessarily require the sending of the debit card to the store manager—who would have to again send it back to the customer—these services are offered to preferred customers by exceptional store managers. Do not expect this to be a part of the service you normally receive from a check-cashing store.

You, too, may be able to bank at a distance and enjoy some of the same conveniences given by commercial banks, without the risk of account seizures, as you control your cash.

ACE issues a reloadable debit card with a MasterCard logo that can be used for depositing and holding your cash, while having the benefits of services similar to a commercial bank account. The temporary card is available for purchase at the ACE stores, and a permanent card is mailed from the account services company, Netspend, some days later. Metabank, a Texas-based online bank, is the sponsoring bank.

Payments for online receipts may be deposited into the account from online payment processors such as www.amazon.com, www.clickbank.com, www.ebay.com, and others. The card can be used for receiving automatic payments from an employer, in lieu of paper checks. And of course, cash may be deposited onto the card at ACE check-cashing stores.

Moneytree

Corporate Headquarters:
Moneytree
P.O. Box 58363
Seattle, WA 98138
Telephone: (888) 604-6669
Website: www.moneytreeinc.com

Moneytree has store locations in California, Colorado, Idaho, Nevada, and Washington. Their website will keep you posted on current store locations and new stores.

The company will cash checks payable to individuals and businesses at rates comparable to the competition.

Users of Moneytree check-cashing stores have reported the stores have reciprocal agreements, which makes it handy for customers spending time in any of the five states where the stores have locations. The swipe of the card provides the man or lady behind the plate-glass window with the information to quickly cash your check, an expedited system, as compared to some company stores that require an individual to gain check-cashing approval from each store within the same corporation.

Quality of service may be dependent on who services you through the plate-glass window. Deal with a regional manager for cashing checks payable to a business.

Moneytree issues a reloadable debit card that may be used for certain banking purposes, including cash deposits, ATM withdrawals worldwide, and automatic deposits or withdrawals via Automatic Clearing House (ACH)—and accounts are managed entirely online.

The debit card is called the Cash Solutions card, which has a Visa or MasterCard logo and is sponsored by Stillwater National Bank, based in Stillwater, Oklahoma.

NEWS ITEM: Moneytree issues a prepaid Visa debit account through Stillwater National Bank in one's name without a Social Security Number requirement. The card has no aggregate limit. Automatic Clearing House transactions, direct deposits, cash deposits, cash withdrawals, and wire transfers via Western Union are account features. A routing number and account number are provided to account holders. The maintenance fee is a flat $9.95 per month, or fees are accessed per transaction. This information has been verified with multiple managers at Moneytree prior to going to print.

Check City
Corporate address:
Check City
P.O. Box 970028
Orem, UT 84097
Telephone: (866) 294-4672
Fax: (866) 430-8030
Website: www.checkcity.com

Check City has store locations in Colorado, Maryland, Nevada, Utah, and Virginia. Store addresses may be checked on the website at www.checkcity.com

Checks payable to individuals and businesses are cashed by Check City. Managers who can make decisions pertaining to the cashing of business checks are supposed to be onsite, and this is an advantage for businesspeople.

This company offers a reloadable debit card that may be used for the bank services we are discussing. Netspend is the issuer, and Metabank is the bank sponsor for the program.

An important point to remember as you seek services with your privacy in mind is that your individual communication and negotiation skills play an important part in the services you are able to receive. For instance, a privacy advocate reports via e-mail that she and her husband operate an Internet business while selling retail products through several websites. They have products they have developed and are affiliates for other companies' products.

This lady searched for a bank account that would allow for their money to be as private as possible. Commercial banks in the U.S.A. all wanted their Limited Liability Company Employer Identification Number (EIN), which they did not have. Additionally, all signers (husband and wife) would be required to provide their Social Security Numbers to the bank. Some of the banks advised they would run credit checks on each signer.

This husband and wife team had registered their LLC privately through the use of the Trust Manager Principle[2] and had assurance that their business privacy was secure. They did not want to compromise their money or banking secrecy, as far as the business was concerned, and expected they were at risk of doing this if a commercial bank were used to process their checks received from online payment processors—www.ebay.com, www.clickbank.com, www.amazon.com, and others.

They inquired at several check-cashing stores and discovered the reloadable debit cards' multiple uses and were advised of the features available through this method of banking.

The couple advised me through e-mail that their attempts to omit their Social Security Numbers from the reloadable debit card account intended to serve as their business bank account failed. However, as this was a primary requirement for their privacy, they persisted and began negotiations with a regional manager. This manager was open to discussing the possibilities of meeting their service requirements, so far as privacy was concerned. He advised them that those who did not have Social Security Numbers provided two forms of foreign identification documentation, such as a Mexican Matricula Consular Identification and a driver's license. He further reported that the company entered either a part of the identification documents' numbers or randomly selected a number for their foreign customers (illegal aliens) who cashed their employer checks. All of this was done with the cooperation and knowledge of the card-issuing company and the bank holding the funds.

When the couple addressed the obvious double standard, store-level managers had failed to acknowledge the difference as being prejudicial or biased. Only when they began speaking to a higher level of management at this same check-cashing service did they begin to make headway in receiving consideration for their privacy requirements.

The regional manager suggested that the signers could eliminate their Social Security Numbers from their reloadable debit cards. Instead, an agreement was made to provide their passport numbers in lieu of the SSN, while including their company name and the first initials and last name of each signer on the cards issued.

Today this family business is operated online privately, the receipts received through checks, money orders, and automatic deposits (third-party credit card processors) are cashed at the regional manager's check-cashing service, and no company tax identifiers (EIN) or personal tax identifiers (SSN) are associated with their accounts. They also have the option of depositing cash into the debit card account as checks are cashed.

As this was a case of particular interest to me, the couple shared some of their personal details regarding their privacy needs.

Apparently, the husband had been hauled into court by a greedy ex-wife twice a year, like clockwork, in an attempt to receive more alimony money and additional child support for two children from a previous marriage. His bank accounts—both business and personal—had long ago been cleaned out by court judgments regarding these matters. He had a desire to continue to support his ex-wife and children but without the privacy invasions to which he had previously been subjected when investigators found his money in commercial bank accounts. The account he now had with the debit card would withstand any asset search, as his Social Security Number was not on the bank records. Further, he and his wife took extra precautions to avoid any possibility of an account seizure, by withdrawing cash from the account immediately upon the receipt of the funds through the automatic clearinghouse (ACH), or whenever other forms of deposits were made into the account.

As this couple proved, negotiation skills matter when a high level of financial privacy is desired. This husband and wife team managed to do it through their use of excellent communication skills and persistence.

Illegal aliens have reportedly been opening these accounts, as well as bank accounts without SSNs, for some years.

Dollar Financial Group

Dollar Financial has operations in twenty-eight states, the District of Columbia, Canada, the United Kingdom, and Ireland, and does business under the names of Money Mart, Loan Mart, and Money Shop.

The following contacts will steer you toward offices that will service you in a number of locations:

United States:
Corporate Headquarters:
Dollar Financial Group
1436 Lancaster Avenue, Suite 300
Berwyn, PA 19312, U.S.A.
Telephone: (610) 296-3400
Fax: (610) 296-7844
E-Mail: info@dfg.com
Website: www.dfg.com

Canada:
Dollar Financial Group
401 Garbally Road
Victoria, British Columbia, Canada V8T 2K1
Telephone: (250) 596-5211
Fax: (250) 595-0410

United Kingdom:
Dollar Financial Group
Castlebridge Office Village
Kirtley Drive, Castle Marina
Nottingham, England NG7 1LD
Telephone: 0115 943-7400
Fax: 0115 934-7444
E-mail: moneyshop@dfg.com

The Dollar Financial Group is a multi-country company that operates under various store names, as indicated above. The clear advantage of this company is the availability of check-cashing service stores in Europe, Canada, and the United States.

Certain traveling business people have advised me of their satisfaction with this company, while enjoying a reasonable level of banking secrecy. The company regional managers are reportedly the best source for quick approval of the cashing of business accounts, at least in the U.S.

While the reloadable debit card sold by the Dollar Financial Group of companies is sponsored by the Illinois-based Suburban Bank and Trust, the card can be used anywhere in the world. However, U.S. citizens cannot load the card with cash in Canada or the United Kingdom—other countries where Dollar Financial Group has a presence—but instead are restricted to making deposits in the U.S. only.

A man from Great Britain wrote me explaining that his bank account was mistakenly garnished by the child maintenance agency. The seizure of bank accounts and homes of men deemed to be in arrears has been occurring in Britain,[3] and this may be justified for those legally obligated to pay child support. Big Bureaucrat's mistakes of fingering and wrongly accusing innocent individuals causes a hardship to men who are not guilty of charges against them due to a mistaken identity[4].

Once again, the clear advantages of using a check-cashing store, in combination with an anonymous safe or safe deposit box—or a prepaid debit card bank account opened with the high-level privacy tactics explained herein—become evident and will prevent abuses of bank account freezes or seizures.

True banking secrecy can be accomplished when an anonymous safe deposit box or a safe is used to store your business or personal cash. How can a totally anonymous safe deposit box be obtained? How does one manage their cash receipts or savings, using a "money safe"? What precautions must be taken when such a banking secrecy program is used? These and other questions are answered in detail, along with a list of recommended money privacy resources, in the next chapter.

SUMMARY

1. Check-cashing stores are the new banks of choice for the astute, aware, privacy-conscious individual or business manager.

2. These businesses are not expensive, as compared to business bank account fees, and there is no risk of having a bank account frozen or seized, as the "cash and carry" method provides for the immediate conversion of checks, business or personal, into cash.

3. Insist on speaking with an area manager or regional manager for the purpose of cashing checks payable to a business.

4. Appropriate business documentation and personal information will be required. All information necessary for cashing checks is negotiable.

5. This chapter references establishments that provide these services in the U.S., Canada, and the United Kingdom.

6. Certain individuals and business managers have cashed business and payroll checks at check-cashing services without providing their home addresses, home telephone numbers, driver's licenses, Social Security Numbers, or Employer Identification Numbers prior to cashing business or personal checks.

7. Banking through the use of a reloadable debit card with the Visa or MasterCard logo may have bank secrecy advantages. The account-sponsoring bank is typically located in a different state than where the retail banking customer purchased the card. Also, less privacy-invasive information will be required to open the reloadable debit card accounts than will be required of banking customers who open bank accounts with commercial banks.

8. Become an expert communicator, and you will be best equipped to deal with these institutions.

NOTES:

1. Grant Hall, "The Money Privacy Crisis; 'Banking' Secretly in the U.S.A.," January 5, 2010, http://www.lewrockwell.com/orig10/hall-g2.1.1.html.

2. Grant Hall, *Privacy Crisis: Identity Theft Prevention Plan and Guide to Anonymous Living* (Las Vegas, NV: James Clark King, LLC, 2006), www.PrivacyCrisis.com.

3. "Child maintenance agency moves to seize 340 non-payers' homes," Guardian.co.uk, February 7, 2010, http://www.guardian.co.uk/society/2010/feb/07/child-maintenance-houses-seized.

4. VodPod, "Man wrongly accused of being a 'deadbeat dad,'" YouTube.com, February 21, 2010, http://vodpod.com/watch/3095884-man-wrongly-accused-of-being-a-deadbeat-dad.

♦ SIX ♦

Safe Deposit Boxes and Safes

"Whoever wishes to keep a secret must hide the fact that he possesses one."

—Johann Wolfgang von Goethe, Author and Playwright

SAFE-KEEPING RESOURCES

Through the use of check-cashing services that provide you with immediate clearance of business and personal checks, you can bypass the use of commercial banks, if you so choose. When you take possession of your cash without placing it on deposit with a bank, you will need a safe place to store it. Essentially, there are three broad categories for keeping cash under your control: commercial bank safe deposit boxes, private companies renting safe deposit boxes, and safes owned by you and installed on your rented or owned property.

Each option has advantages and disadvantages for banking secrecy.

24/7 Private Vaults

In 1999, Mr. Elliot founded 24/7 Private Vaults in Las Vegas, Nevada. A world-renowned privacy expert, Mr. Elliot heads a top-notch management team that is open twenty-four hours a day, seven days a week, and 365 days a year.

Your privacy is assured at 24/7 Private Vaults, as no identification, tax identification number or Social Security Number—not even a name—will be required to open a completely anonymous safe deposit box.

Visit them at:

24/7 Private Vaults
3110 E. Sunset Road
Las Vegas, NV 89120 U.S.A.
Telephone: (702) 948-5555
Website: www.24-7privatevaults.com

Das Safe

Europeans and others who prefer Austria as a strategic location can have password-protected privacy storage of valuables at Das Safe. Hours of operation are from 8:00 A.M. to 8:00 P.M., Monday through Friday, excluding public holidays.
Contact Das Safe at:

SAFE Wertfachvermietungs ges.m.b.H.
Auerspergstrasse 1, A-1080 Wien, Austria
Telephone: + 43-1-406 61 74
Fax: + 43-1-408 49 76
Website: www.dassafe.com
E-Mail: info@dassafe.com

BANK SAFE DEPOSIT BOXES

Banks in the U.S. offer safe deposit boxes for storing valuables, and privacy and separation of personal assets and company property may be obtained, when a separate legal entity is used to hold the box.

A Nevada Limited Partnership or a Nevada Limited Liability Company, with you as the manager and signer, will mean that the entity, not you, is the safe deposit box holder.

Banks will want the EIN of the partnership or LLC, as well as other company documentation that proves the company is a legal entity, as well as your government-issued primary identification. This will mean you will necessarily have to provide a copy of your passport or driver's license to the bank, a form of secondary identification, and probably your Social Security Number. Certain privacy seekers have been known to convince bank managers to waive the inclusion of the EIN and/or SSN on the account records.

Make certain to register the entity using the Trust Manager Principle, as described in my first book, *Privacy Crisis: Identity Theft Prevention Plan and Guide to Anonymous Living* (www.PrivacyCrisis.com). When a company is registered properly, utilizing the Trust Manager Principle, the manager will remain anonymous, and your name will not surface on officer and company searches done through the database of Nevada-registered companies.

Will your name—as the manager and signer on the bank safe deposit box held by the partnership or LLC—come up during an asset search? That depends of the sophistication of the database used by the investigator, the budget allocated for the asset search, as well as how the bank titles the holders of their safe deposit boxes. And since searches are done by state, not nationally, the searcher will have a more difficult time finding the box, when it is held in a small bank or credit union far away from where the hunted is known to spend his or her time.

If you are a manager and signer on a Nevada Limited Partnership–owned safe deposit box at a bank, and your personal assets are being searched, this company-owned box, with you as signer and manager, should not be affected. You manage the partnership and sign on behalf of the partnership and are not the legal owner of the box contents. However, courts and banks could do any number of things to grab assets believed to be owned by one subject to a lien or judgment. You decide what is best for you, in view of all future potential risks.

Banks will normally require your business as an account holder prior to issuing a safe deposit box to the partnership or LLC. For example, if the limited partnership checking account is held at a given bank, you can open a safe deposit box under the partnership name at the same bank or a branch location.

One privacy angle used by a certain privacy advocate is to hold a non-interest-bearing checking account in the name of a trust, of which he is the signer, at a particular bank. Through this account, he was able to rent a safe deposit box, though the box was held by the limited partnership, a different entity than the trust, of course. A search of all bank accounts would not normally uncover the safe deposit box held by the partnership under these circumstances.

RECOMMENDED BANKS FOR HOLDING SAFE DEPOSIT BOXES

Belize Bank
60 Market Square

Belize, Central America
Telephone: (501) 227-7132/227-7082
Fax: (501) 227-2712
E-mail: bblbz@belizebank.com
Website: www.belizebank.com

Any Number of U.S. Banks

Properly register an entity for holding assets for privacy and become the signer and manager for this entity.

For instance, a Nevada Limited Partnership may be used to hold assets. The bank safe deposit box can be held in the partnership's name, with you as the signer authorized to access the box.

HOME SAFES

The dangers of having a home safe are well documented. *In Cold Blood,* by Truman Capote, detailed the murders of the Clutter family by Dick Hickock and Perry Smith. These murderers learned of the rumor of the home safe through a prison contact who had worked for Mr. Clutter.

Many who desire privacy will choose the home safe, as they trust neither banks nor businesses that operate secure safe deposit box facilities. Others will not want the inconvenience and expense of the travel and time associated with an offsite safe deposit box.

For those who insist on having a safe in or near their home, secrecy is of paramount importance, as is the selection of a money safe that will withstand several hours of fire. Generally, this level of quality means a safe that weighs more than you do and is moderately expensive. Many who opt for this total control and immediate access to their safe's contents insist on paying cash for the safe, transporting it to their business or home, and installing it in total secrecy. And all of these decisions are wise ones.

If you're entirely sure you want total banking secrecy, you will want to take control of your cash and cash equivalents by storing these valuables in your private safe or safe deposit box. The risks are obvious. A fire could in theory wipe you out, as could thieves—those working for "you know who," or the more common variety—and your life and livelihood may be threatened as a result of the loss.

That being said, total peace of mind is never achieved entirely while living beneath the radar. Risks are an inherent part of the business of privacy, and it always costs more to protect yourself than to live as do the masses—unless and until you wake up one morning and learn your business or personal accounts have been frozen or seized or have had a lien placed on them. Then, you may wish you had used the total control method of an anonymous safe deposit box or safe.

STORAGE CONTENTS

Common contents of safes and safe deposit boxes include foreign and domestic currency, gold, silver, rare coins, diamonds, bonds, other precious metals, precious stones, jewelry, money orders, insurance policies, automobile titles, property deeds, computer data, business entity documents, family heirlooms of all types, and other keepsakes, documents, and valuables.

A statute may make it illegal to store cash in a bank safe deposit box. Check on this prior to storing cash in a bank vault.

ANONYMOUS GOLD PURCHASES

Years ago, gold bullion purchases could be made anonymously through any number of companies. Privacy was an advertised business feature of buying and selling gold, and I did it myself without anyone on the other side of the counter knowing my name and without any paper trails except for my nameless receipts.

Somewhere along the line, the gold and rare coin dealers were put under pressure to collect names and other privacy-invasive information on their customers. Except for a few, that is.

As of this writing, two companies that are valuable resources for your private gold purchases and foreign currency purchases are California Numismatics and Associated Foreign Exchange.

California Numismatic Investments

It's been many years since I visited this store, and I'm happy to report they're still in the same location and have the same "cash and carry" policy they have had for years, as per a call to their office just prior to this book going to print. Walk in, tell them what you want, provide cash as payment, and walk out. Your privacy is assured.

Contact California Numismatic Investments at:

California Numismatic Investments
525 West Manchester Boulevard
Inglewood, CA 90301-1627
Telephone: (800) 225-7531
Fax: (888) 443-4653
Website: www.golddealer.com
E-mail: info@golddealer.com

Associated Foreign Exchange

This company has been located at the same location for many years, and you may buy foreign currency from them with monetary limitations and without any paper trail whatsoever. AFEX also sells gold bullion.

So for foreign currency necessary for travel, as well as for moderate-sized purchases, Associated Foreign Exchange, Inc. can be used as a resource. Business can be completed at a distance, and large transactions can be made, when the sacrifice of personal and company information is provided.

Contacts are:

Associated Foreign Exchange, Inc.
433 North Beverly Drive
Beverly Hills, CA 90212
Telephone: (310) 274-7610
Fax: (310) 274-6167
Website: www.AFEX.com

BUYING FOREIGN CURRENCY FROM BANKS

The money center banks will sell foreign currency to you for a hefty commission. Certain regional banks will be able to supply your currency needs, as well. You will need to have an account at the bank, in nearly every case, to make these purchases. However, you can use the *Public Trust Account*, as described in *Privacy Crisis*, with its low balance, as a "reference account" or other business account and pay cash for your Swiss Francs, Japanese Yen, Euros, GB Pounds, Canadian Dollars, or other currency you choose to buy. Or you can have the amount of the purchase debited from the account you hold at the bank selling the currency to you.

The foreign banks listed as resources in this book will be able to purchase foreign currencies to be held in a foreign bank account, and the purchase of foreign currencies in the form of Electronic Traded Funds (ETFs) can be made through stock brokerage firms listed herein.

The purchase of foreign currency and private storage of this currency is equivalent to holding a foreign bank account, without the risk of seizure or confiscation, and serves as a hedge against further U.S. dollar devaluation, in my experience.

SUMMARY

1. Private safe deposit boxes are offered by companies in the U.S. and Austria.

2. Bank safe deposit boxes held under an entity name that is properly registered using the *Trust Manager Principle*[1] offer a high degree of privacy.

3. Home safes offer convenience, and it is imperative the safe be concealed and be kept secret.

4. Anonymous precious metals purchases are possible through the use of cash as payment for coins and bullion. Certain companies provide private purchase options for precious metals and foreign currency.

5. Foreign currency held in a safe or safe deposit box may be a hedge against further currency devaluation and be a valuable asset that can be held privately.

Notes:

1. Grant Hall, *Privacy Crisis; Identity Theft Prevention Plan and Guide to Anonymous Living* (Las Vegas, NV: James Clark King, LLC, 2006); www. privacycrisis.com.

SEVEN

Banks and Stockbrokers

""The threat of people acting in their own enlightened and rational self-interest strikes bureaucrats, politicians and social workers as ominous and dangerous." "
—W. G. Hill, Author

SERVICES: THE WAY THINGS OUGHT TO BE

During the 1980s, I had a personal banker at a U.S. money center bank assigned to me as I managed a business. He would meet with me on a walk-in basis and was available to discuss any aspect of the business services offered by the bank, including the easily obtainable merchant account. Banking, with many American banks at that time, was easy and convenient.

Many bank managers' desks were positioned in the middle of the banking floor space, and they would personally handle anything requested. I recall one explaining the details of the bank wiring system, personally taking care of a foreign bank wire transaction, and phoning me the minute the procurement was completed. What a great era of customer service it was!

Stockbrokers were so efficient and knowledgeable during this same period of time that I can recall having my questions answered by a brokerage firm's staff day or night, twenty-four hours a day, seven days a week, without exception. Supervisors were never called into discussions, I was never placed on hold with music, and I was never advised someone would have to call me back for answers to my inquiries. It was a great time to be a customer. I miss it.

Seldom do I use the telephone for contacting brokerage houses or banks today—generally, a complete waste of time. In fact, service is so substandard in the U.S., particularly within the financial services industry, that one will find it difficult to justify using the telephone at all.

For banks and brokerages to use under-skilled, part-time personnel and an automated system to run their businesses is not cheaper. Far from it. In fact, I guarantee it is more expensive. Many, like me, would gladly pay a yearly maintenance fee, were we given decent customer services, as were afforded *all* customers two or three decades ago.

Foreign banks in well-known offshore investment havens were so efficient during the 1980s and 1990s that they would take calls after business hours to service their American customers. Personal bankers were assigned to clients of these banks, and they would perform a variety of services above and beyond the call of duty, sometimes without generating fees to justify these services at the time.

However, the foreign bankers realized the value of providing satisfaction to the customer while sometimes sacrificing the immediate gratification of payment for these services. If certain foreign banks did not normally offer a requested service by a customer, some would do it anyway, on the spot, without supervision or policy change. They just did it. They wanted your business and could have cared less what an American bureaucrat thought of their banking secrecy laws—sacred contracts, now in a ruinous state, imposed on the traditional international banking centers by the fascist-like war machine known as the United States of America.

NON-TRADITIONAL BANKING

As described in Chapter 5, a business manager or individual may be well served to bypass traditional bank accounts offered by commercial banks and instead opt for using a reloadable debit card sponsored by the banks cited in that chapter.

A distinct privacy advantage may be gained through the use of these accounts, due to the nontraditional nature of the accounts and the distance often placed between the customer and the bank associated with the debit card/bank account.

Please review Chapter 5 and make inquiries to the appropriate companies to satisfy your unique business and personal questions about these accounts.

ACCOUNT-OPENING INFORMATION IS NEGOTIABLE: CONSULT MANAGEMENT

In all cases, the astute business manager, investor, or individual will want to speak to the highest-level manager possible at a given financial institution prior to and during the account-opening process. That may be a tall order to accomplish, as today, banks, brokerage companies, and check-cashing stores alike have installed contact shields for most management that matters, and your efforts to make good contacts with higher management will, for the most part, be difficult to accomplish.

Still, I have found that making contact with a regional or area manager, not store or branch managers, to become a time saver in the long run. And often, getting the name of such an individual—followed by calls to their office—has facilitated the process and the meeting of my financial "account" objectives and goals. You may want to start with contacting such a manager, as well, when you begin the important process of opening a bank or brokerage account.

FOREIGN BANKS

Many foreign banks do not provide guarantees of banking secrecy and confidential investment services to U.S. residents, as they did a couple of decades ago.

The once-sacred secret Swiss bank accounts have gone by the wayside, thanks to pressure applied by the United States. Likewise, the Austrians dropped the ultimate banking secrecy account, the Sparbuch, a bearer type of passbook account that was as anonymous as currency itself. Even Liechtenstein, the smallest German-speaking country in the world and the location where the Swiss reportedly once stored their money, has come under scrutiny, and many tax evaders' accounts have been uncovered in recent years.

Generally, those banking havens that still offer a high degree of secrecy by law or constitution have changed and are now in the Caribbean, Central America, or South America. Specifically, they can be found in Nevis, Belize, and Panama, along with the tiny south sea island paradise, the Cook Islands. However, Americans cannot have bank accounts in the Cook Islands, except through the use of a legitimate loophole that will be explained later.

FOREIGN BANKING RESOURCES

These institutions are known to offer the privacy seeker some opportunities for holding assets and doing business offshore:

Belize Bank
60 Market Square
Belize City
Belize, Central America
Telephone: (501) 227-7132/227-7082
Fax: (501) 227-2712
e-mail: bblbz@belizebank.com or onlinebanking@belizebank.com
website: www.belizebank.com

Belize Bank offers a variety of banking services to businesses and offshore customers who are willing to take the time to open an account. Expect to spend a good deal of time gathering recommendations, documents, and information for the satisfying of the foreign account-opening requirements.

The documents may include, but are not limited to: a notarized copy of a passport; company registration papers from the Secretary of State where the business is located, for business accounts; a bank or brokerage referral letter; a letter of reference from a lawyer; and a history of your business operations.

Tax identifiers for businesses and individuals are not a requirement for a foreign account at the time of this writing. However, one or both may be required to open a merchant account that is linked to the business checking account.

Belize banking secrecy is some of the best in the world, so the effort may be worthwhile.

As of this writing, however, there seems to be no convenient way of privately accessing funds from a distance, as the plan to implement a debit card tied to a foreign account has not been accomplished, though that service is supposed to be a future bank account feature available to foreigners. Of course, residents of Belize and visitors to the country can accomplish their banking needs in person. In addition, a network of twelve automatic teller machines (ATMs) is positioned throughout Belize for all Belize Bank customers.

A merchant account can be established for offshore account holders who sell products and services, and while the reserves are naturally kept high for these merchant accounts, the ability to accept Visa and

MasterCard through an offshore account in a jurisdiction with banking secrecy is a valuable service.

A bank account in the name of a Limited Liability Company registered in Nevada or Nevis are both viable options for business banking secrecy. These accounts have been opened entirely by mail and fax. However, the approval process can take a substantial amount of time, and it may behoove a business manager to appear in person with documentation in hand or following the submission of these documents through courier services.

Investment services are offered to high-net-worth individuals and business investment accounts.

Belize Bank is a worthwhile foreign bank resource for investments and business privacy purposes.

Capital Security Bank Limited
P.O. Box 906
ANZ House
Rartonga
Cook Islands
Telephone: 682-22-505
Fax: 682-22-506
E-mail: info@csb.co.ck
Website: www.capitalsecuritybank.info

Capital Security Bank Limited, a Cook Islands–based bank, has historically not made accounts available to American citizens. However, those who have relationships with their subsidiary company, Southpac Group, may qualify in certain cases. For example, clients who use the offshore trust services of Southpac may have an account opened by a trustee—either the offshore trustee or the trustee at home—and may have access to a personal and confidential bank account and/or investment account through these channels.

Through the use of trusts and business entities in various jurisdictions, Americans may qualify and be eligible for banking and investment services, and it may be advisable to make contact with either Capital Security Bank or Southpac Trust Limited for information pertinent to your individual and business needs, as the Cook Islands offer exceptional banking and investment privacy for holding accounts there.

Southpac contact information is as follows:

Southpac Trust Limited
P.O. Box 11
ANZ House
Avarua, Rarotonga
Cook Islands
Telephone: +682 20 514
Fax: + 682 20 667
E-mail: enquiries@southpacgroup.com
Website: www.southpacgroup.com

U.S. BANKS

By and large, traditional money center banks in the U.S. offer a wide variety of services. Privacy is negotiable, and I have discovered it matters a great deal *who you are,* as well as who you deal with at a given bank. Certain bank managers are more interested in providing personal and business banking services than others, in my opinion.

Privacy is not generally part of the package, but a number of privacy advocates still accomplish reasonable levels of privacy as they use these institutions for personal and business banking services. For instance, many U.S. banks have been used to establish bank accounts held by trusts, Limited Liability Companies, and Limited Partnerships. Certain signers and managers on these types of accounts have used the trust or company Employer Identification Number (EIN) only, while not including their Social Security Number on bank records. However, generally speaking, banks almost always insist on the signer's SSN when they open a business bank account or a trust account.

You may, through persistence, find a bank manager who will accommodate your banking privacy needs.

Certain regional and local banks may be more amenable to your privacy needs, while still being able to provide the same services as the huge money center banks.

This bank has a reputation for providing good customer service:

Thrivent Financial Bank
2000 E. Milestone Drive
Appeleton, Wisconsin 54919-0006
Telephone: (920) 628-3451
Website: www.thrivent.com

Thrivent Financial Bank has additional locations in Missouri, Illinois, and Minnesota.

STOCK BROKERAGE FIRMS

Only a handful of brokerage firms offer customer service that is acceptable to one accustomed to first-world business standards.

These companies are known to have fine services for investors:

TD Ameritrade (U.S. Accounts): www.tdameritrade.com
TD Waterhouse (Canadian Accounts): www.tdwaterhouse.com

TD Waterhouse and TD Ameritrade provide a full spectrum of services to clients in the U.S., Canada, and other countries. Most of the account services are accomplished online or via telephone and fax, though some cities have offices as well at the time of this writing.

Accounts may be held by individuals, trusts, and a variety of business entities.

Though high-level privacy is difficult to accomplish with a U.S. stock brokerage firm, the use of a Nevada Limited Partnership, as fully described in this book (Chapter 10) enables one to control assets and manage investments and capital while it is owned by another entity, an ideal way of making certain an individual owns nothing and controls everything.

While the inclusion of a manager's or signer's Social Security Number on the limited partnership account is not a legal requirement, as per my last consultation with a legal expert on this subject matter, most stock brokerage firms will insist on it anyway. Why? Because the level of ignorance is so high within the financial services industry in the U.S. today that managers and others are told to gather up all possible information in order to "know your customer." Knowing your customer is fine and dandy, but most individuals designated as application takers have no idea what it means, and in order to cover themselves and prevent repercussions from higher management, they attempt to gather all information possible about you in order to please someone else sitting in an ivory tower who *does* make the application-approval decisions.

Based on the fear instilled in the stock brokerage houses by government agencies, I suggest a personal touch be added to the application process. This may mean sitting down with a manager in an office and completing the application, while whoever approves it is available by telephone and at the ready to field questions when the local manager cannot answer your simple questions—questions about requirements for opening the limited partnership account or other entity account that will be holding the brokerage account that you, as the signer and manager, will control.

This due diligence will prevent the "underwriter" in the ivory tower from kicking the application back to you via snail mail three weeks later and holding up your account-opening process. When you sit down and complete the application in person with the office manager's boss standing by at his/her phone, you can exercise your discretion by refusing to provide the information they want, if you believe it to be too privacy-invasive for your taste. Furthermore, you can avoid having the brokerage company retain both personal and business documents required to open the account *if* they refuse to open the account for reasons unknown to you during the personal meeting. And of course, Mr. or Ms. Ivory Tower will not take phone calls or be available to discuss anything with you—after all, you are *only* the customer.

Keep in mind, you will no doubt run into resistance as you attempt to obtain only basic services, as described above. Most brokerage offices and banks are staffed with part-time clerical-level individuals who are either new to the business or are so undereducated, underachieving, and underconfident that when even routine questions come up, they will rudely interrupt your meeting or telephone conference to phone or flag down a "supervisor" to ask them what to do.

To the experienced businessman or businesswoman accustomed to making business decisions on a day-to-day basis, it is absolutely appalling to watch the American workforce in action today, and the incompetence is nowhere more evident than in the financial services industry. Prepare for it.

Wachovia
www.wachovia.com
Telephone: (800) 922-4684

Wachovia is now a Wells Fargo company and provides a complete line of stock brokerage services that are available to the individual or business.

investorseurope
745 Europort
Gibraltar
Telephone: +350 200 40303
 +1 (214) 556-6382
 +44 203 283 1469
 +5 (21) 02-2698
Fax: +350 200 51795
E-mail: info@investorseurope.net
Website: www.offshorestockbrokers.eu

European and American investors and others may open accounts with investorseurope. Their reputation at the time of this writing is for good customer service and fine executions, and they come to me recommended by investors who have used their services for trading and holding brokerage assets offshore.

MERCHANT ACCOUNTS

The ability to accept Visa, MasterCard, and other credit cards as payment for purchases is paramount for today's businessperson. And the banks and other companies that offer merchant accounts will want all the information normally required of a bank account, plus a personal guarantee from the owner or controller of the business. Moreover, a substantial amount of money will be kept in reserve, unavailable for use in most cases, to assure the integrity of the merchant account.

How then does a privacy seeker/businessperson with intentions of total honesty meet these requirements, while preserving his or her business and personal privacy?

For those with a substantial sales history, an offshore merchant account tied to the business account at the Belize Bank, as previously referenced, or another bank with similar, high-level privacy guarantees may be the answer, as privacy invaders who attempt to track down the controller, manager, or owner of such a business account will surely be thwarted—unless it can be proved that laws are being broken or about to be, according to my contacts at this bank.

Foreign bank account maintenance fees and merchant account fees will be more expensive than for U.S. banks, so you will have to weigh the value of your business privacy against the costs involved.

THIRD-PARTY PAYMENT PROCESSORS

For those without a sales history and who still require a credit card processor, a third-party payment processor may be ideal. A number of companies process payments for a percentage of the sale and provide other services to the businessperson. For instance, Amazon (www.amazon.com), ClickBank (www.clickbank.com), and other popular online vendors offer exposure to products being sold by businesses online through their high-profile websites, and they process the credit card payments.

As per U.S. statutes passed in 2011, all who sell online are tracked and traced by name and taxpayer identification number. No longer can substitute tax identification numbers be obtained from nominee directors who agree to stand in for those wishing to retain their privacy. In view of this new law, following due diligence and persistence, we discovered that through the use of our private company registration procedures, as explained in chapter 10, Nevada Limited Partnership, and illustrated in Figure V., Privacy Crisis Private Company Registration, we have been able to keep our business and personal privacy while still being in compliance with all requirements of online payment processors. We accomplished this by obtaining tax identifiers for both the trust, the manager of record (Trust Manager Principle), followed by obtaining an Employer Identification Number for the entity being managed by the trust.

Accounts with the online banks associated with the debit cards listed in Chapter 5 (check-cashing stores) can serve as the bank for receiving deposit receipts generated from online sales. Or checks may be issued payable to the business; these checks may be cashed at the check-cashing stores mentioned in Chapter 5 or at a check-cashing service of your choice.

GIFT CARDS

Nearly everyone needs to use a credit card for certain online purchases and other shopping. Cards with the Visa and MasterCard logos and others are readily available at your supermarket and other retail outlets. These cards are preloaded and cannot be reloaded and may be purchased in amounts of $25 to $100, in most cases.

One important feature of gift cards is the ability to register them in any name you choose, in order to preserve your privacy while making online purchases.

Two cards that offer higher balances that may be convenient for your use are the following:

www.acecashexpress.com

ACE offers a preloaded gift card with amounts up to $250, and you may pick one up at a store in your city. Visit the website above for information on convenient locations near you.

www.simon.com

Simon Property Group, Inc. sells gift cards up to $500 to retail customers. Visit their website for information on how to find a store carrying these cards in your area.

While gift cards may be used for online purchases, they have limitations and cannot be used for renewal purchases.

The gift cards listed above have been used successfully for credit cards to secure an account, in the event customers who buy online return the merchandise to the online company that processes the credit card payment. This is a huge advantage over using a personal or business credit or debit card, both from a privacy standpoint and in terms of the amount of money that is accessible when a dispute occurs.

SUMMARY

1. Reloadable debit cards provide a degree of banking secrecy, combined with the convenience of online banking with additional banking services. Check-cashing stores market these cards to their customers. Refer to Chapter 5 for details.

2. Foreign banks may be of use for business and personal banking, as well as for investors who require high-level money privacy. Certain banks continue to offer valuable privacy options for customers, business and personal, worldwide.

3. U.S. banks provide full services to customers; a degree of privacy can be accomplished when dealing with some of these banks and bankers.

4. Investors can use a Nevada Limited Partnership to hold assets under their control at stock brokerage firms, and this entity can be privately registered, as per the information in this book. Please refer to Chapter 10 for details on the Nevada Limited Partnership.

5. Merchant accounts held at some foreign banks may be ideal for the privacy-conscious businessperson. Third-party processors may be valuable for those without a long sales history.

6. Gift cards registered under an alternate name preserve privacy for online purchases and other uses.

♦ EIGHT ♦

Offshore and Domestic Banking: Considerations and Preparation

"Research, preparation, and negotiation skills are keys to establishing a high-level financial privacy program, and all will serve privacy advocates well as they establish The Ultimate Bank Secrecy account, or other banking privacy measures, and exercise their rights to financial privacy."

—Grant Hall, Author, Business Manager

WHY YOU MAY NEED OFFSHORE BANK SECRECY AND ASSET PROTECTION

D o you need bank secrecy for your business or investments? If so, you may decide that offshore banking is the correct choice for your circumstances.

Successful privacy advocates recognize the value of banking privacy for both business property and personal holdings.

Government seizures of business and personal property occur frequently. Currency devaluations and government debt seem to overshadow rights to privacy and constitutional laws and may make assets and bank accounts more vulnerable to government agency seizures.

NORFED assets were seized after nearly ten years of operations, and the "Soviet-Style Attack on NORFED"[1] demonstrates how business assets are seized and questions and answers about the constitutionality of the seizure are delayed, *unless and until* the case gets to court. Once a seizure occurs, huge legal fees may be required, and the defendant will have to win the case to reclaim the property.

A properly formed offshore asset protection structure for a business entity doing business in the U.S.A., complete with a foreign business bank account and/or investment account, may prevent assets from being seized in the first place and may make it illegal for the seizing agency to keep the property—IF laws are respected and followed, that is.

OFFSHORE BANK ACCOUNT REQUIREMENTS

Offshore banks will require in-depth information about their prospective banking client. Those who desire offshore banking privacy may be asked to provide these specifics and documents prior to their bank account being approved by the institution:

▶ Name, address (business and personal), telephone numbers, and e-mail address.

▶ Domestic bank or brokerage account information, with account average balances and a contact person at the institution.

▶ Copies of utility bills.

▶ Professional references who vouch for the character of the prospective banking client (examples: attorney, accountant).

▶ Copies of government-issued identification, duly notarized.

▶ Other personal or business information, as per the institution.

Offshore bank account opening procedures may take some time to complete, as all reputable banks will want to verify new client information prior to opening an account.

OFFSHORE BANKING ADVANTAGES

Removing assets from "business unfriendly" jurisdictions—especially the "seizure happy" U.S.A.—seems like a prudent move for businesses and high-net-worth individuals and others who can benefit from offshore banking privacy, in the opinion of this author.

Furthermore, when business assets and personal funds are held in an offshore bank account, the agency, company, or individual who attempts to seize these assets will be asked to demonstrate the reason for the seizure, and this reason must be congruent with the laws of the jurisdiction where assets are kept. In certain jurisdictions having "true bank secrecy," only criminal cases warrant the seizure of assets. The assets have to be discovered prior to such an action being brought forth, and this discovery may be indeed difficult when banking privacy is combined with high-level financial privacy principles.

PROTECTED DOMESTIC COMPANY

Keep in mind that having domestically formed entities is a huge advantage for doing business at times, and a business bank account in the U.S.A. is sometimes a requirement for receiving funds for payment for services and goods sold, with certain online payment processors, for example. Similarly, a company domiciled in the U.S.A. may be a requirement in certain instances, as well. So going offshore for normal business banking services, for a domestic company, may get in the way of doing business.

Companies have accomplished their asset protection objectives and investment goals by having their business entities based in the U.S.A. but owned by offshore entities—an Offshore Asset Protection Trust, for example—based in a foreign country known to provide protective measures to businesses that require their holdings be kept free from seizure. Nevis and the Cook Islands are two countries sometimes used for the purpose of forming Offshore Asset Protection Trusts to own assets of U.S.–based companies.

"BANKING PASSPORTS" AND WHY NEVER TO USE ONE

I grew up reading a number of privacy books whose authors wrote about escaping greedy ex-wives and their money-grubbing attorneys, or other undesirable people or circumstances many of us have to deal with during crisis periods in our lives. These authors touted the virtues of living under the radar on sandy beaches in faraway places, to escape the shafting penalties handed down by courts to "innocent" plaintiffs. And mentioned within these fairy tale paragraphs were stories of how "so and so" had purchased the ultimate remedy to stave off the enemy— a "banking passport" from an offshore "broker" who sold bogus passports issued by defunct countries. Please don't fall for this out-dated, worn-out scam. Provide true and correct information to financial institutions which meet your business needs and privacy requirements.

Upon reflection, the stories of luring the gullible escapers of reality to their new promised land with unidentifiable money—disguised through a fake passport issued by a country that had its name changed—seem more outrageous today than when I first read of these tales some thirty-odd years ago. I imagine there are far more failures than successes concerning the use of phony passports sold for banking purposes. Don't participate in these frauds. Such tactics may provide Big Bureaucrat, in any number of jurisdictions, with all the ammunition he needs to seize your assets and throw your ass in jail pronto.

Treat offshore banking as you would any new business venture. Do your research, prepare your application(s), gather your references, make contact with prospective institutions, and be honest and truthful about yourself, your business, and your requirements—and you will do fine.

FOREIGN BANKING INTRODUCTIONS

I've never been introduced to a foreign banker by a third party but have met several over the course of many years. Most of the time, you will do as well or better by rowing your own canoe, as you seek to do business with an offshore bank. And while the Internet is full of companies that promise such introductions, most have little to offer that you cannot accomplish solo. In fact, when you go it alone, you gain a whole new perspective as you prepare the paperwork and make the written, telephone, and physical contacts. And you're certain to keep all of your offshore business confidential—right down to the institution(s) you work with, as you establish a banking or brokerage relationship in a foreign jurisdiction.

BANKING NOMINEES; NONSENSE FROM NON-EXPERTS

Not much has changed since my writing and speaking campaigns against the use of banking nominees, first exposed in late 2006. That's when *Privacy Crisis,* first edition, was published, and I've followed up with my comments on the subject during interviews on talk shows since that time. Always, I have advised against the use of having someone else be in control of your assets, the one and only exception being when one is disabled and cannot make his or her own decisions. But to use another to control money for privacy purposes is a bad idea— an idea formed without the full benefits associated with study, time, and experience with experts and the practical application of using bank secrecy in real time while under fire, as I had to do once in my life. And I used the same entities, with the same structures, outlined in this book and *Privacy Crisis*. Doing so, I managed to escape unscathed and without spending one thin dime on legal costs for a matter that could have resulted in substantial costs, had the structure to prevent the damages not been in place and had I not had the knowledge base of privacy living to make myself "invisible." And the best part is that all of my "defenses" were not only legal but recommended by two counselors of law.

BEARER SHARES

High on my list of "do not do's" is the establishment of bearer shares, used to make the company owned by one who possesses the stock certificates. Imagine losing them or having them stolen. You don't need to resort to these types of movie-style make-believe tactics to have bank secrecy.

Being the possessor of bearer shares of companies registered in countries whose constitutions claim bank secrecy is not a worthwhile procurement, in my experienced opinion.

Why risk the loss of bearer shares—they are the same as currency? Besides, the once stalwarts of bank secrecy, Switzerland and others, have recently succumbed to pressures from U.S. bureaucrats to relinquish account holders' banking information for the sake of the tax receipts claimed to be owed, or other claims. And neither the bank nor the bureaucrats who order the disclosure of the once-private holdings care how the shares of the company holding the funds are held. If they're hunting for money, and they convince the bank that promised bank secrecy to let them go on a fishing expedition in the large pond of the bank's customer database, if they find someone believed to being a tax delinquent, they try to grab the money.

Regardless of where you go to bank, use entities to hold your funds, register them privately, and do all offshore business according to the laws of all jurisdictions involved—and that includes filing necessary forms with the Internal Revenue Service concerning foreign bank accounts or other tax agencies that require your full disclosure of any and all foreign holdings.

HOW TO MAKE YOURSELF AND YOUR MONEY INVISIBLE

This is do-able. Of course, there is a steep price to pay in terms of the costs in time, effort, travel expenses, and money to accomplish such a high level of privacy, as well as the emotional costs of the stresses to do it and keep that level of privacy over the long term.

As explained earlier in this book, foreign banks may not be your best choice for the ultimate in money and property secrecy. Instead, the check cashing stores in both the U.S.A. and abroad, combined with the debit cards with associated online bank accounts, can provide the ultimate in bank secrecy, when extreme privacy measures are applied.

The stalking victim interviewed in a previous chapter provided examples of what some have decided to do to make themselves and their money vanish. I do not recommend that you follow these leads, however. Also, the use of cash and anonymous safe deposit boxes or safes for holding the currency provides secrecy of holdings, with only the holder of the assets as a secrecy variable. Are you ready for this kind of stress?

Some, like the stalking victim mentioned, may feel they have no choice but to live almost entirely as another person, to escape far greater stresses and dangers, and if your circumstances are of this nature, certain offshore banking and financial institutions may warrant your consideration, as well as domestic companies, as explained in this book.

NEW IDENTITY FOR BANK SECRECY

Becoming a new person on paper, with a new identity, can be accomplished the legal way. To become a citizen of a foreign country is possible—change your name and be issued a new passport under the new identity. However, as explained in *Privacy Crisis*, "first world passports" cost a great deal of money and/or take years to obtain. Do you have years to make an identity change? How about the money it may take to shorten the wait? If so, over time, a *new you* can become established on paper, with a new identity and a new foreign passport. And along with the new identity, an extremely high level of bank secrecy can be accomplished, as your new name becomes the foundation for establishing banking and investing relationships with financial institutions.

OFFSHORE BANKING AND THE "ULTIMATE BANK SECRECY ACCOUNT"—A COMPARISON

Considering the aforementioned business seizure case of the NORFED Corporation—and others that can be discovered through Internet searches and that have occurred to both businesses and individuals—

what defensive strategy must be put in place by a business manager in charge of the company assets or a controller of a high-net-worth individual's assets, in order to withstand seizure attempts by government, court orders, or others? And which structure is best—an offshore asset protection structure, or a domestic plan with the foundational bank account being what I have coined the *Ultimate Bank Secrecy Account.*

Let us draw comparisons between two such accounts for illustration purposes, while utilizing known foreign and domestic banking resources, as described and listed in this book.

The resources provided have been used to set up bank secrecy accounts for individuals and businesses. Verification that the resources have been used for individuals and business entities, as described in this comparison, has been made prior to this book going to print.

FOREIGN BANK ACCOUNT

Hypothetical theory-laden ideas concerning something as important as money and banking secrecy are not productive. Let's deal with specifics, in this comparison of foreign banking with U.S. banking resources, as far as bank secrecy is concerned.

Foreign banks listed in this book as resources for bank secrecy will want all the information mentioned in the sub-chapter heading of *Offshore Bank Account Requirements,* as described earlier in this chapter. The fact that these references are required and have to go through various communication channels to reach the bank account representative results in some losses of personal and/or business privacy. You never know how many law clerks, legal assistants, bankers, brokers, or other office personnel store your contact information with a foreign bank, as you innocently try to gather references as account opening requirements. Add possible e-mail, fax, and telephone communication to the mix, and you have a strong potential likelihood of having your most important personal and confidential data being intercepted by some bystanders at home, not to mention the customs guys who inspect your courier-generated package full of notarized passport copies or your application for that foreign "secret account," and you're sure to be discovered and possibly marked as a "person of interest" even *before* you step into the batter's box. Of course, you can thwart the efforts of all this discovery by traveling to that foreign land with paperwork in hand and hope you have it right, when you finally arrive. Either way, opening a current account—a bank account for a business or for personal use—is

:h a huge deal, once you learn what you are up against, and I have
ed foreign bank resources that will serve your needs.

Remember that a current account for business purposes or personal
use is best handled under another entity name. An LLC based in Nevada or Nevis will work fine for business purposes, although the Nevis LLC may present obstacles for doing business in the states, in certain business circumstances. A multitude of other choices are available,
as well. Base your entity decisions on your business requirements and
seek advice from counsel or your accountant. Concerning a personal
account, using one's true name is not advisable. An offshore trustee
for the Offshore Asset Protection Trust can work, in conjunction with
your trustee at home, to coordinate the opening of a bank account,
when you are already a client of Southpac or other company that forms
asset protection trusts. In any case, such a relationship will provide you
with the shields to make a high-level bank secrecy plan do-able.

Investments can be kept in a variety of offshore entities, or a Nevada
Limited Partnership can be used, while the offshore asset protection
trust owns the partnership. Investments are a separate subject, and this
comparison is for only the business or personal current bank account,
with bank secrecy as a primary objective.

Clearly, with private entity registration—either in Nevada, as I describe in *Privacy Crisis,* or offshore, using a registration company to
register foreign trusts or LLCs—the business manager or individual desiring banking privacy can accomplish this objective. Maintaining the
secrecy will be difficult to impractical. And what is so special about an
offshore bank account, anyhow? You can accomplish bank secrecy using the methods described next, and with the resources provided in
this book. In addition, the institutions are more practical to use and
just as secret as the foreign institutions today, and the exceptions, are
for the traveling business man or lady who spends a reasonable amount
of time offshore. Then an offshore current account may be advanta-
geous and most convenient.

DOMESTIC BANK ACCOUNT (PREPAID DEBIT CARD, ONLINE BANK ACCOUNT)

Bank secrecy with a domestic bank, equal to any foreign bank account secrecy, is available today, *when the account is set up correct-
ly using the resources in this book.* I call this type of account the *Ultimate Bank Secrecy Account.* This account is not understood by those

proclaiming to have financial privacy expertise, because it is dependent on human variables, in part, though not entirely. And this type of account is not absolute, its conditions varying from institution to institution and from manager to manager. However, I have adequate testing completed on this type of account, and while each institutional manager may not meet a privacy advocate's highest privacy requirements, some have and do. This domestic account is providing customers with bank secrecy, with substantial bank features and advantages not available to foreigners who bank offshore, not to mention the greater convenience of managing the account completely online, *without* a messy paper trail of bank statements or other common commercial banking records.

With prepaid debit cards bearing the Visa or MasterCard logo sold by check cashing stores (see Chapter 5), a bank account for individuals or businesses can be established, and banking privacy can be accomplished.

Certain managers of businesses have purchased the card from institutions referenced in this book and used the online bank account tied to the card for business purposes. The card has been held in the name of individuals and/or business names, at the discretion of the store manager selling the card. If you want this card for business purposes, please be candid with the store manager or regional manager about your business needs, and perhaps he/she can accommodate your business. Substitute numbers have been used in lieu of the Social Security number and Employer Identification Number.

Regardless of whether the account is for personal or business use, the account—which becomes an online personal bank account or a business account—can be an untraceable account, when it is set up properly. In-depth communication and research has been completed on this account. Certain stores may be unaware of the flexibility of the higher-level management of their own company or the financial institutions managing the bank accounts for the sponsor banks. But recognize that your job is to find management who wants your business and has the respect to provide the banking services you require individually or as a manager of the business account you set up with the institution.

Further, store managers at institutions referenced in this book have guaranteed that these accounts can be opened without any tax identifier whatsoever—a huge privacy advantage by itself. More than one store manager voluntarily advised me that the *Ultimate Bank Secrecy Account* would withstand bank database searches, due to its being inside the financial walls of the financial services company structure or

PERSONAL BANKING SECRECY PLANS

1.) Check cashing store(s), personal online bank account, no SSN, debit card bank sponsor
or
2.) Check cashing store, anonymous safe deposit box, money safe, no bank account

Receipts: ACH deposits (online bank account), Employer checks, third party checks, money orders, cash.

Cash checks, money orders at check cashing store(s), withdraw cash, ATM's.

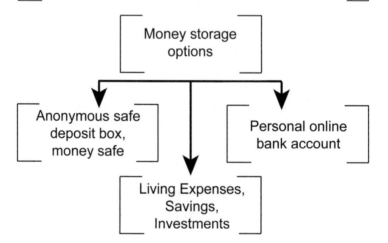

Money storage options

Anonymous safe deposit box, money safe

Personal online bank account

Living Expenses, Savings, Investments

Personal money management, bank secrecy plans, U.S. bank, check cashing stores, safes and safe deposit boxes.
• Figure II

nestled deep within the corporate account database, depending on the company. And in either case, these types of accounts are *not* held on the banking books of commercial banks as customer accounts—business or personal—and will surely withstand private investigator database searches, especially when the privately registered business name is used to open the account —and the account is maintained under this fictitious name *without* Social Security numbers, employer identification numbers, home addresses, mothers' maiden names, and the like—common commercial banking data used as identifiers.

ACTUAL CASE STUDY: ULTIMATE BANK SECRECY ACCOUNT

Jay and Marge manage a privately registered, Nevada Limited Liability Company, which holds websites used to market proprietary products and sell products developed by others as affiliates.

The manager cashes checks received from the business operations at various U.S.-based check cashing stores.

A business bank account was needed to receive online payments for those companies that do not issue paper checks, as well as for holding business receipts until excess cash could be withdrawn for capital expenditures or investment purposes. This account was to be used as a current account only. The company managers use third-party credit card processors only and have no immediate plans to secure their own merchant account.

Management at a check cashing store referenced in this book agreed to open the prepaid debit card bank account in the name of a business name, while using company registration numbers and identity document numbers in lieu of Social Security numbers or employer identification numbers.

The company name is a name that could also be used as a person's name and is registered as an LLC with an anonymous manager (trust manager principle).

Management at the check cashing store where the prepaid debit card was purchased required the managers' names, addresses, phone numbers, and copies of U.S. passports, and these records were retained by the store. The bank account was opened with the company name only, and substitute SSNs and EINs were used for privacy and security of the account, as per the customers' requests.

This account is used for cash deposits, cash withdrawals at many

ATMs, and for receiving online payments from third-party credit card processors, and the account is managed entirely online. A bank routing number and an account number is provided for this account. The only banking features not included are the ability to write checks and to receive and send wire transfers. For bank secrecy, neither of these services are recommended, and this management used MoneyGram and Western Union for wire transfers and paid bills with money orders, prepaid debit cards, or cash.

This *Ultimate Bank Secrecy Account* is as secure as any current account ever offered by Swiss banks at any time in recent history, based on my experience with Swiss banks.

Bank secrecy has been obtained through the use of a financial institution—a check cashing store—which has a bank sponsor that provided the customers with the banking resources of this sponsor bank. This is an ideal business banking privacy plan for U.S.-based businesses.

ULTIMATE BANK SECRECY ACCOUNT

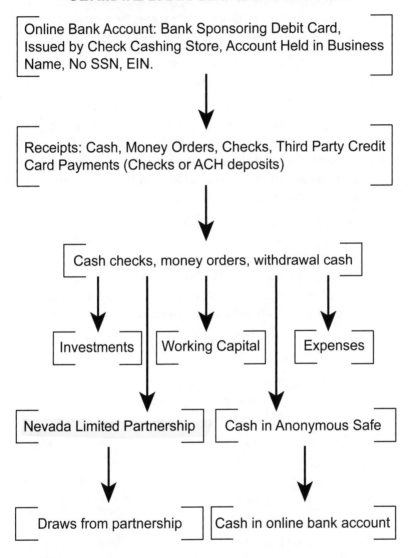

Online Bank Account: Bank Sponsoring Debit Card, Issued by Check Cashing Store, Account Held in Business Name, No SSN, EIN.

Receipts: Cash, Money Orders, Checks, Third Party Credit Card Payments (Checks or ACH deposits)

Cash checks, money orders, withdrawal cash

Investments

Working Capital

Expenses

Nevada Limited Partnership

Cash in Anonymous Safe

Draws from partnership

Cash in online bank account

Money flow options from the Ultimate Bank Secrecy Account, U.S. Bank. Signer is known only to the bank.
• Figure III

SUMMARY

1. Business seizures and other asset confiscations by government and others warrant offshore asset protection plans that may include offshore bank accounts for privacy and protection.

2. Offshore asset protection trusts may protect assets by owning U.S.-based Nevada Limited Partnerships. Protection is the primary goal.

3. Offshore bank account requirements for business and personal accounts are stringent, and the honest and complete disclosure of all identity documents and personal and business information to the foreign bank is recommended. Do not defraud institutions in any jurisdiction.

4. Both offshore and domestic current accounts are worthy of consideration for the business manager seeking bank account security and privacy. U.S.-based businesses may have their business entity protected through an Offshore Asset Protection Plan. A protected domestic company may have more business friendly characteristics than a foreign company.

5. Do not provide phony identification or "banking passports" to financial institutions.

6. Do not use nominees for banking secrecy. Power of attorney over money and assets is appropriate for one who is disabled and unable to make his/her business decisions.

7. Certain companies provide introductory services for the purpose of opening foreign bank accounts. Foreign and domestic banking resources in this book can be contacted directly for the purpose of financial and banking services.

8. Bearer shares are perceived as the ultimate in asset secrecy, as whoever possesses the stock certificates has control of the company—including bank and brokerage accounts and other assets. Loss of bearer shares is equivalent to losing cash. Private registration of companies, as described in the Privacy Crisis series of books, provides for anonymous control of a business.

9. Bank secrecy has various levels of privacy. Make choices based on individual and business circumstances. Though it

is possible to have total banking secrecy, this necessitates going to extreme measures of privacy living and expense to maintain this level of banking privacy.

10. A legitimate new identity, complete with a new passport to support the new name, will take three to five years or longer, as well as expenses related to relocation, travel, and other diligence, to become a citizen of a first-world country. A new identity and citizenship provides the foundation for the highest level of bank secrecy.

11. Individuals and business managers will find advantages and disadvantages to using foreign and domestic financial institutions for their current account needs. The ultimate bank secrecy account, as described, provides the individual or manager of a business with the highest level of bank secrecy.

NOTES:

1. Jacob G. Hornberger, "The Soviet-Style Attack on NORFED," *The Future of Freedom Foundation*, November 7, 2007, http://www.libertydollar.org/commentary/pdfs/1196746715.pdf.

NINE

Invisible Home Mortgage

"Money is usually attracted, not pursued."
—Jim Rohn, Entrepreneur and Author

HIDDEN DEBT FOR PRIVACY

Many people who value privacy want to purchase homes. This section will provide a way for one to borrow money for a home purchase without exposing the reason for the borrowed money, as well as keeping the home location confidential.

Traditional home mortgages are privacy-invasive loans and require the inclusion of far too much personal information for the taste of those seeking privacy, and the traditional borrower will be subjected to the continuation of credit bureau file monitoring.

Payment record history will be posted to the database files of multiple credit bureaus, and all who view the homeowner's credit bureau files will be privy to their home address. And since mortgages are readily bought and sold, multiple financial institutions, their personnel, and all others who peek at your loan paperwork will be aware of where you live.

Privacy seekers should avoid a traditional home mortgage and are advised to borrow money discreetly. This section will provide a method of purchasing a home privately while borrowing *all* or a portion of the principal loan amount. When one has the borrowing power to purchase property this way, what I refer to as an "invisible home mortgage" can be created and will enable one to live under the radar.

BORROWING WITH COLLATERAL

Please remember to make certain to borrow only according to the provisions of your credit agreements with lending institutions.

When borrowing against property, liquid or illiquid, the astute privacy-living manager's objective is to make the source of funds used to purchase the home "invisible."

This method of borrowing funds is the exact opposite of how the masses borrow money. In fact, once a home mortgage is secured, borrowers have provided all who access key credit bureau information with a telescopic view of their financial life and portions of their personal and business lives, as well.

Property that borrowers use for collateral, with the objective of establishing an invisible home mortgage, may include a margin stock brokerage account, rental real estate property, or other property deemed suitable for collateral by a lender. A combination of asset classes may be collateralized, as well.

Businesspeople who have followed guidelines as described in *Privacy Crisis* utilize business entities to hold property. These entities may be used as collateral for the individual who desires to create the invisible home mortgage.

The Loan Case Studies A and B described below are theoretical and are not based on actual cases.

LOAN CASE STUDY A:
LIMITED PARTNERSHIP HOLDS LIQUID ASSETS

A stock brokerage account held by The High Desert Stream Limited Partnership is managed Bob Bouldersenz.

As manager of the partnership, Bob decides to borrow $155,000. He has full control of the brokerage account in the partnership's name—currently, $459,000. A partnership meeting is held with Bob presiding, a loan agreement is made, Bob calls his broker, and the next day, the margin loan money is wired from the brokerage account to The Blue Sea Breeze Trust checking account—a bank account of which Bob is trustee and signer. Bob now owes The High Desert Stream Limited Partnership $155,000.

Being a creditworthy borrower, Bob has excellent credit and several unsecured credit lines in his personal name that have been used as needed over a period of time. Today, he calls bank number one for the purpose of accessing a non-secured personal line of credit available at one point over the prime rate. As he has checks for this purpose, he advises banker number one's account manager of his intention to write a check on this infrequently used line of credit. The check is written for the full account balance of $100,000, payable to High Desert Stream Limited Partnership, and deposited into the bank account of the partnership. A remaining balance of $55,000 exists on the original loan from the partnership to Bob. A $100,000 debt has been incurred by Bob to bank number one.

Bob's next telephone call is to bank number two, the bank that has made a business line of credit available to Bob in his name at a point above the prime rate, in the amount of $60,000. Today, he is going to use it to pay off the balance of the loan to the partnership. Bank number two's account manager mails the check for $55,000, Bob receives it in three days, rubber stamps it "for deposit only," and into the Blue Sea Breeze Trust checking account it goes. Once bank number two's check clears, Bob writes a check for $55,000 to High Desert Stream Limited Partnership. The balance of the partnership loan is now zero. Bob has incurred an additional debt of $55,000 and owes bank number two this amount.

The loan to the partnership has been paid with two separate bank loans secured at competitive rates, due to Bob's high credit rating and excellent payment history on previous loans. A total of $155,000 remains in the Blue Sea Breeze trust account.

Bob makes an offer on a three-bedroom, two-bath, corner-lot house for an amount just under the $155,000 list price, which is accepted. Money from the trust account is used to buy the home for cash.

Bob's credit bureau files are frozen, and only those who have issued him credit may see these files. As payment due dates occur each month on the two loans with bank number one and bank number two, Bob pays principal and interest on each loan. Those who view Bob's personal credit bureau files see loan payment records to bank number one and bank number two.

Bob Bouldersenz has borrowed 100 percent of the money needed to purchase a home, and no one has any idea what he did with the money. Bob has created an "invisible home mortgage."

LOAN CASE STUDY B:
LIMITED LIABILITY COMPANY HOLDS
ILLIQUID PROPERTY

Betty Howorthing manages an apartment complex as an onsite manager. She is ready to turn her management duties over to another manager and live offsite in a single-family home. An LLC that Betty manages and controls owns the rental properties.

Betty has her sights set on purchasing a home currently valued at $160,000, and she desires to leverage rental property under her control to buy this house.

Sleep Easy Living, LLC, the owner of the apartment building under Betty's control and management, has been issued an equity line of credit in the amount of $250,000 by Mercantile Corner Street Bank and Trust. As manager, Betty decides to borrow the amount of $160,000 from the equity line of credit.

Sleep Easy Living, LLC holds a company meeting with manager and secretary Betty presiding; a loan in the amount of $160,000 is made to Betty. The loan amount of $160,000 from the company checking account is deposited into The Scattered Pecan Grove Trust checking account, of which Betty is trustee and signer. Sleep Easy Living, LLC now owes $160,000 to Mercantile Corner Street Bank and Trust. Betty owes $160,000 to Sleep Easy Living, LLC. A portion of the value of the LLC-owned apartment is now in cash, in the form of a secured equity line of credit.

Betty's resource choices to pay her debt to Sleep Easy Living, LLC include low interest rate and promotional balance transfers offered by four credit companies. She has an exceptional credit history, and her past responsible borrowing gives her a preferred credit customer rating with certain financial institutions.

She negotiates balance transfer interest rates with four separate credit card companies and receives interest rates below the prime rate for the life of the loan on each of the credit card accounts.

The credit card companies issue checks to Sleep Easy Living, LLC for the entire balance of Betty's debt of $160,000.

Betty is now in debt to four separate financial institutions and begins to pay principal and interest payments on each account monthly as the due dates occur. As a privacy-living individual, Betty's credit bureau files are frozen, and only a few creditors are able to view her credit bureau reports, outstanding balances, and payment history.

The $160,000 loan to Betty from Sleep Easy Living, LLC remains in the Scattered Pecan Grove Trust checking account. Betty makes a cash offer for a three-bedroom, two-bath house. Her offer is accepted, and no one has any idea how she funded this purchase while creating an invisible home mortgage.

Lest you have questionable confidence in theoretical models of high-level privacy loans, as described in Case Studies A and B, valuable reader, I am going to reveal an actual case study of an invisible home mortgage—my own. The following event actually occurred, and I certify it as such.

INVISIBLE HOME MORTGAGE: ACTUAL CASE STUDY

While using a margin loan from a stock brokerage account held by an entity under my control, I borrowed an amount equal to 100 percent of the value of a property I expected to buy. Of course, I documented the loan from the entity to me personally through the proper meeting, and internal company paperwork was properly completed, as well. The funds were deposited into a bank account held by a trust of which I am the signer, and I am a trustee of the trust holding the bank account.

I negotiated an interest rate of 4 percent for the life of the loan with a major financial institution. The source of funds was a single, non-secured credit line. I owed the entity for the money loaned to me and advised the institution providing the personal, non-secured loan to pay the entity directly and in full for the amount of my debt. A check was issued, as per my instruction.

Money borrowed from the entity holdings remained in the trust checking account, and I used this money to buy a home for cash.

An invisible home mortgage was created.

As the 4 percent loan guarantee was in place, I was not in a hurry to pay it off, as it was a competitive rate, and my payments to the financial institution were timely and exceeded the minimum due each month for a period of time. However, I eventually concluded that paying off the balance in full was prudent, and this was done.

SECRET HOME OWNERSHIP

Once you have managed to finance your home privately, your next hurdle is the private registration of the property with the county where the property is located.

Forming a trust to own the home—with a trustee who agrees to sign on county records, as well as insure the home—will make the home anonymous as you prepare to live in your future residence. Your attorney is a good choice for this role as trustee, as he or she is bound by law to keep your affairs confidential and can be disbarred if this attorney-client privilege is breached. The attorney can resign as trustee once all the insurance and title issues are properly recorded, and this agreement to resign duties can be signed at the time the trust is formed. Then you, as successor trustee, can begin to live as an anonymous resident in the home—without a trace to your true identity.

Obviously, you will need to take precautions as you live in your new trust-owned home *if* you intend to remain anonymous. How serious are you about living privately? Do you have family members who will have to be educated about your proposed lifestyle? This can be done, when you and your spouse are truly dedicated to living secretly for your privacy, protection, and security.

In order to make certain that your security is not compromised as you live in your home, the use of alternate name(s) is imperative, as is the proper registration of the automobile(s) used by all family members.

Complete privacy guidelines used by successful privacy experts for all aspects of privacy, including the home and automobile, may be found in my first book, *Privacy Crisis: Identity Theft Prevention Plan and Guide to Anonymous Living.*

"INVISIBLE HOME MORTGAGE"

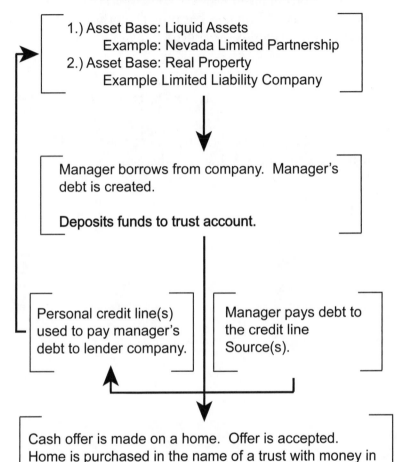

1.) Asset Base: Liquid Assets
    Example: Nevada Limited Partnership
2.) Asset Base: Real Property
    Example Limited Liability Company

Manager borrows from company. Manager's debt is created.

Deposits funds to trust account.

Personal credit line(s) used to pay manager's debt to lender company.

Manager pays debt to the credit line Source(s).

Cash offer is made on a home. Offer is accepted. Home is purchased in the name of a trust with money in trust checking account.

Personal credit reports reflect debt owed by the manager to institution(s) that paid company loan.

INVISIBLE HOME MORTGAGE: debt structure prevents anyone from knowing source of funds used to buy a home.
• Figure IV

SUMMARY

1. A type of collateralized loan I've coined "The Invisible Home Mortgage" Principle has provided privacy-conscious people with secrecy as they borrow money for home purchases.

2. Detailed descriptions of theoretical loans and the author's actual "Invisible Home Mortgage" facts are included in this chapter.

3. A home may be owned secretly, when a trust is used for owning the property as described herein.

TEN

Nevada Limited Partnership

"I'd like to live as a poor man with lots of money."
—Pablo Picasso

PRIVACY FOR LIQUID ASSETS

A Nevada Limited Partnership, also known as a Family Limited Partnership, is the preferred entity of many privacy-conscious investors for holding liquid assets and offers privacy and asset protection.

A general partner or partners have a percentage of ownership and maintain control of the partnership. General partner(s) are also held responsible for any liabilities that may be incurred by the limited partnership.

Who are the general partners? Typically, a partnership is formed with the husband and wife as the general partners and the children being named as the limited partners.

A Nevada Limited Liability Company may be formed for the purpose of being the general partner of the Nevada Limited Partnership. The LLC will be given a minority interest in the partnership of 1 percent, an amount that would limit the liability of the general partner(s) to this small general partnership interest.

CREDITOR PROTECTION

"Limited partnerships are effective for asset protection because, under Nevada partnership law, assets that are held in a limited partnership are not subject to attachment or execution by a partner's creditors."[1]

Shifting personal ownership of assets to a limited partnership provides for the ability to "own nothing and control everything" and is an ideal shield for protection from creditors—*when* the timely transfer of assets is made into the partnership, of course.

If one has no knowledge of any future claims against him/her, then the transference of personal holdings into a properly formed limited partnership will withstand the test of fraudulent conveyance.

ANONYMOUS MANAGEMENT

Do you want to remain anonymous as you manage your liquid holdings? Keeping snoops out of your business is possible, when you properly register the partnership holding title to your property. I have outlined these steps in detail, in *Privacy Crisis: Identity Theft Prevention Plan and Guide to Anonymous Living*.

Key privacy principles and concepts include the *Trust Manager Principle*—a key to avoiding any discovery of the true manager(s) of the business. The trust is listed on Secretary of State records as the manager of the partnership's general partner. The general partner, LLC is listed by name on the partnership registration filing. Trusts have no registration requirements with the Nevada Secretary of State, and when combined with the signature of an administrative trustee, whose only authority and duties lie in signing on documents on behalf of the trustee(s), anonymous management of the partnership is accomplished.

BANK AND BROKERAGE ACCOUNTS

Financial privacy can be achieved through the use of a Nevada Limited Partnership with a financial institution, to the extent that *only* the bank or brokerage company has details concerning who is controlling the business entity. For instance, Bert and Betty Zinnzobb are the trustees of The Whole Life Garden of Freedom Living Trust, an entity that requires no registration anywhere. The trust owns Andrews Rigland, LLC, the general partner of Collins Biggs Limited Partnership, the entity used to hold the liquid assets under the control of Bert and Betty, who are the limited partners of the company.

PRIVACY CRISIS PRIVATE COMPANY REGISTRATION

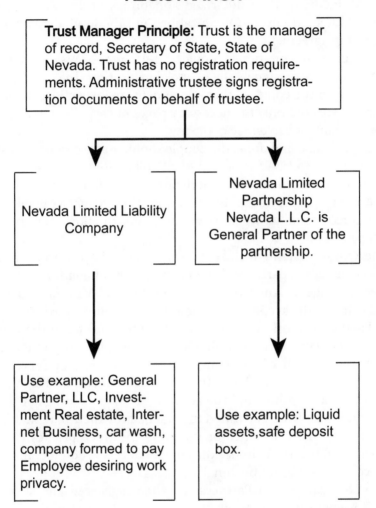

Trust Manager Principle: Trust is the manager of record, Secretary of State, State of Nevada. Trust has no registration requirements. Administrative trustee signs registration documents on behalf of trustee.

Nevada Limited Liability Company

Nevada Limited Partnership Nevada L.L.C. is General Partner of the partnership.

Use example: General Partner, LLC, Investment Real estate, Internet Business, car wash, company formed to pay Employee desiring work privacy.

Use example: Liquid assets, safe deposit box.

Private registration through the use of the Trust Manager Principle provides anonymity for management.

• Figure V

A stock brokerage firm or a bank will want to see the supporting documents verifying that the couple has control of Collins Biggs Limited Partnership. This documentation will include certain portions of the trust, including their notarized signatures as trustees, the general partner LLC's Articles of Organization, and the limited partnership's partnership agreement.

Once all documentation is provided, certain portions of these documents may be requested by the financial institution. The couple should not provide entire copies of these documents to institutions but should selectively sort out only the necessary pages of each document category for the bank or brokerage company.

After all is said and done, the couple should make certain to instruct the institution to title the account as "Collins Biggs Limited Partnership" and exclude any mention of their names as limited partners from the account title. However, they will want their names available to the institutions' personnel when they request information about the partnership account.

The account statement and debit card(s) associated with the account should contain the partnership name *only*, without mention of the controllers/managers/signers of the account, Mr. and Mrs. Zinnzobb.

All who see the account statement will have no idea who is in control. Further, even if someone were to track and trace the account back to the Zinnzobbs—an unlikely happening, in view of their anonymous registration of the company with the Nevada Secretary of State—no harm will be done. They control, manage, and sign on behalf of the partnership, and the account or other holdings of this entity cannot legally be garnished or attached for their personal liabilities. So even if an investigator uncovers the thick privacy layers in place around the assets under the control of this prudent couple, they can expect to suffer no personal damages.

The Nevada Limited Partnership, when registered and structured with privacy in mind through the use of the Nevada LLC as general partner, combined with the Trust Manager Principle,[2] contains two important features demanded by privacy advocates who have assets: secrecy and protection from creditors.

SAFE DEPOSIT BOXES

Safe deposit boxes can be held in the name of a limited partnership. When these are rented from commercial banks, expect to provide similar documentation for storing valuables as you would when opening a bank account.

In certain cases, a privacy advantage can be gained when the manager of a limited partnership has another account with the financial institution (a business bank account in the name of an LLC, for example) and requests a safe deposit box to be rented in the name of the partnership under his or her management at a different branch.

In any case, the care to register the partnership anonymously with the Secretary of State should provide a sufficient layer of secrecy for holding the safe deposit box. Even when the bank manager requests all personal identity information from the signer/manager of the partnership, the partnership's hard assets stored in the box should not be in jeopardy, regardless of any future claims brought against those signing on behalf of the business entity that owns the assets. I say, "should not" and advise you that in today's environment, constitutional rights are being ignored by those claiming to rule over you. In view of this trend, a bank safe deposit box may not be safe enough for you, but holding it in a name of an anonymously registered Nevada Limited Partnership is about as safe as you can get.

OFFSHORE TRUSTS

Some who are the designated managers and limited partners of a Nevada Limited Partnership believe an extra layer of protection to be necessary. For those, an Offshore Asset Protection Trust (OAPT) may be used.

Preferred jurisdictions for the OAPT include Nevis, the Cook Islands, and others. One reputable company providing trust services is listed below:

Southpac Trust Limited
P.O. Box 11
ANZ House
Avarua, Rarotonga
Cook Islands
Telephone: +682 20 514
Fax: + 682 20 667
E-mail: enquiries@southpacgroup.com
Website: www.southpacgroup.com

ASSET PROTECTION ADVICE

The purpose of this book is to enlighten readers on financial and banking privacy principles and concepts, not to provide legal advice or other professional recommendations.

Please address all questions concerning legal asset protection, accounting advice, and tax planning strategies to an appropriate professional of your choice.

SUMMARY

1. A Nevada Limited Partnership has been successfully used by privacy-conscious families and individuals for holding liquid assets. Through the use of a Nevada Limited Liability Company as the general partner, combined with the Trust Manager Principle, the controller(s) can remain anonymous.

2. Creditor protection and privacy are benefits of using the Nevada Limited Partnership.

3. Bank and brokerage accounts and safe deposit boxes may be held by a Nevada Limited Partnership.

4. Offshore asset protection trusts may own the Nevada Limited Partnership, for added protection.

NOTES:

1.. R. Glenn Woods, "Effective Strategies for Asset Protections: Gifts, Exemption, Limited Partnership, and Nevada and Offshore Protection Trusts," Woods, Erickson, Whitaker & Maurice, LLP, 2001–2009, http:www.woodserickson.com/article5.html, http://www.woodserickson.com.

2.. Grant Hall, "Trust Manager Principle; Avoid a Business Privacy Invasion," February 26, 2009, http://www.privacycrisis.com/trust_manager_principle.html.

ELEVEN

Paying Bills Privately

"A man who pays his debts on time is soon forgotten."
—Oscar Wilde, Poet

CREDIT BUREAUS: CORPORATE WATCHDOGS

The credit bureaus' job is to track and trace borrowers of money. Responsible borrowing by adults who are productive enough to make enough money to become worthy credit risks in the first place would seemingly merit normal living and freedom from bother by the lender, but this is not the case. Once you promise to pay the debt, your life as a *normal* borrower becomes an open book to the institution or other credit bureau–subscribing lender providing the funds.

Financial institutions who participate in the Ponzi scheme of the Federal Reserve System simply make a profit or spread—a percentage on the money borrowed from the Fed—and then lend it to their "subjects," who sacrifice more of their "stored labor" (work) as they pay even higher fees (interest) to buy their big- or small-ticket items. Houses, cars, recreational vehicles, and boats are commonly financed, as are the bare necessities, when the consumer becomes shut out of the wage-earning and salary-receiving class to one of financial dependence. As this book is written, a depression is in full swing, and the borrowers are tapping all credit lines for food, clothing, and other essentials to survive.

Once you qualify for a loan to borrow substantial money, you have proven yourself to be a responsible adult with a reasonable degree of earning power. Think you are going to be given the luxury of having your financial affairs kept private between yourself and the bank or other lending company—(after all, you did "qualify" to borrow the money)? No. Once you have signed the note or tapped the credit line, you are treated as a toddler still in diapers, not as a successful businessperson, as Big Bureaucrat's corporate partners, the major credit bureaus—TransUnion, Equifax, and Experian—begin to carefully monitor your payment history and your other business and personal activities, as well. These watchdogs are the hired guns of the banks and other lenders of money and credit—order takers who monitor, watch, and hassle you, through paper mailings and pressure, to ensure you do not become overextended in your borrowing practices with other lending companies or businesses that allow for instant gratification through the financing of consumer goods and services.

You will be watched by banks and credit card companies, the instant debt creators and "family members" of the Fed, lest you become at risk of missing a payment or change to a job that pays less, thereby placing your ability to pay at risk, or you attempt to skip out on the debt entirely.

If you participate as a borrower, as the masses do, you too will be subjected to major privacy invasions by all who work for the credit bureaus, subscribe to their databases, or pay a one-time fee to view your financial affairs.

You have options besides following the masses in their sheep-like trance as they bow to processors of credit—clerks who provide "banking" services from invisible "boiler rooms" in faraway towers of deception—New York, India, Manila—wherever the cheapest subcontractor and script reader can be purchased to process the money from debt fraud that the average American consumer knows nothing about.

CASH

Cash as a means of settling essential bills and other debts stops the paper trail on your purchases. Use it, whenever possible and practical to do so.

What bills and purchases are practical cash purchases? Any item you can think of. In fact, very large-ticket items may be purchased for cash. My Chinese acquaintance advises that she and her family bought their current house for cash. Though this method of payment is not common in the U.S., several readers have written telling me they use *only* cash and money orders.

For years, I have purchased vehicles and other large-ticket items with cash and money orders. And while these types of purchases are extraordinary to certain dealers and sellers, I have never experienced a negative response when cash was used for buying an item.

Be careful while arranging your cash purchases and do not engage in "structuring," or you risk being charged with a crime as you withdraw and spend your own money.

MONEY ORDERS

Buying money orders with cash and using money orders for paying bills provides an anonymous way of settling bills.

Without a link to your bank account, anyone who tries to monitor your life will not have a clue about where your money is kept.

For many years, I have used money orders for paying bills for which it is not practical to pay cash. Money orders are private, negotiable instruments, much like cashier's checks, which were once almost cash equivalents. Today, money orders can be purchased in total privacy, for the most part, and are readily available at numerous businesses, including retail stores, convenience stores, and check-cashing stores.

On occasion, I have been asked for my name when buying money orders. When and if this happens to you, I suggest you not provide a name *if* you want privacy as you pay your bills. Otherwise, the clerk will enter your name into the business database and track your future purchases. Certain check-cashing service businesses have a policy in place to ask for customers' names when they sell money orders. On occasion, I have advised these clerks that privacy is the reason many of us use money orders and providing a name defeats this purpose. Clerks at one such store responded by saying the name and associated money order purchase enables the store to help recover the lost funds if a money order is lost. Obviously, this privacy-invasive ploy has not been well thought out by whoever wrote the company manual, as a cash receipt for the money order purchase and the payment stub is all that is needed for making a claim to Western Union or MoneyGram—two reliable companies that sell money orders through agents. Processing your claim for a lost money order will cost you $15, as of this writing.

When you need a privacy layer as to your location, sensitive bills paid by money order may be re-mailed. Send a note with the bill inside a larger envelope, along with a note attached to your offshore mail-drop nominee, instructing him or her to stamp and mail the bill from that location. Any number of re-mailing services can be found via an Internet search. Bills can appear to have been mailed from a location far from your home location, when a re-mailing service is used. Mr. or Ms. Investigator will be hit with a double whammy, as there will be no clue as to where the money to buy the money order originated from, and your location will be preserved through re-mailing the bill.

Two reliable re-mailing services are:

Texas Re-mail Service
Web: www.texasremail.com

Irish Office
Web: www.irishoffice.com

The inclusion of your name or company name and account number may be necessary for the company to properly credit your bill payment. Writing or typing this information on a separate sheet of paper while using an illegible signature on the money order will leave all pertinent information out of the money order company database.

Keep in mind that since money orders can be traced to the store where they were purchased, as well as to the payee who accepts it as payment for goods and services, a little privacy is sacrificed when using them. Although an investigator could discover your general location on the date the money order was purchased, I learned this is quite difficult and unlikely, according to phone conversations with supervisors at Western Union, a company that sells money orders and provides money wire transfer services.

CASHIER'S CHECKS

The use of a cashier's check enables one to present a negotiable instrument to the payee that is a step closer to cash than personal checks. Fraudsters have reduced the perception of quality of cashier's checks, once deemed cash equivalents.

Today, cashier's checks often require a three-day hold by commercial banks and stock brokerage companies. Check-cashing stores (see Chapter 5) require no hold time, of course, and will give you your cash on the spot. Why the difference? One type of company within the financial services sector does their due diligence to make certain the instrument will clear, while the others choose not to do this in order to use your money during the hold time, with exceptions, of course.

CHECKS

Checks—business and personal—provide an open book to your financial affairs. However, there are minimal risks of privacy invasions and money seizures, when proven privacy protection controls are in place.

The use of the "Public Trust Account"[1] provides for the use of checks and/or deposits in conjunction with an account that maintains a low balance for loss control. A "transient account or pass through account"[2] provides a temporary holding account for funds and increases privacy for the individual or company desiring bank secrecy.

AUTOMATIC CLEARING HOUSE

Electronic payments or debits to and from a bank or brokerage account are known as Automatic Clearing House (ACH) transactions. These credits and debits come and go at the approximate speed of the clearance of paper checks.

The use of the ACH system provides the same records as paper check transactions in an electronic format. Financial privacy is compromised to a great degree, when ACH is used.

BANK WIRES

Bank wires are a faster version of electronic checks and provide immediate credit of funds from any location in the world, once confirmation is made for receipt of the money.

You will need a business or personal bank account to send a wire transfer, and the electronic money trail will be traceable to whatever accounts received and initiated the transfer.

MONEYGRAM AND WESTERN UNION

MoneyGram and Western Union provide wire services without the need for a bank account. Identification will not be required to send money via these sources. However, the receiver of funds will be required to present identification to the agent.

Limitations in currency amounts are placed on these types of wire transfers, and the fees are much higher than wiring funds via the banking system.

Bill payments may be made to vendors accepting these modes of payment. I have never presented identification while paying bills through Western Union and MoneyGram.

CREDIT CARDS

Whenever I have a chance to use other people's money at a competitive rate of interest for a worthwhile purchase, I jump on the opportunity. Come to think of it, I once borrowed money at zero percent interest.

I have made it my business to make certain my debts are always paid on time, and consequently, when business cycle periods justify low interest rates, I have credit lines in place to take advantage of this cheap money.

Writing checks on a credit line tied to Visa, MasterCard, Discover Card, or other lines of credit make perfect sense, when the money you borrow can be obtained cheaply and is used for a prudent purchase. Or you may not have to use a check at all but instead charge the purchase to the card itself.

Whether this borrowed money comes in the form of balance transfers, cash advances, or credit lines offered at very competitive rates, it matters not, as the important consideration is to have access to the funds *when* an opportunity presents itself.

Expect to have higher payments than conventional loans, when credit lines are accessed to fund purchases. However, it is not uncommon for those with superior credit ratings to be offered promotional rates and life-of-loan rates at interest rates below the market value.

Your credit bureau files should be frozen, as per my writings in *Privacy Crisis*.

When your bank or other credit line agreement provisions allow for it, you may disguise purchases so that no one will know your business, much as I once did for a home purchase (Chapter 9) while creating an invisible home mortgage.

Always have a plan for how borrowed money will be repaid. Do borrow responsibly, and recognize that assets of all kinds may depreciate following your purchases.

If you believe your account number has been shared, misused, or kept by a vendor following the use of your credit card or credit line, a phone call to a manager at the issuing financial institution is usually all it takes to change the number, and this move will prevent the abuse of your account.

I do not recommend the use of credit cards for the payment of routine bills; i.e., groceries, gas, personal supplies, and the like. Instead, I prefer using cash for these purchases.

DEBIT CARDS

Debit cards are tied to a bank account under your control and may be necessary for certain uses. Certain car rental companies will not accept these, I understand. I do not like the idea of anyone knowing the source of my funds and would not use debit cards unless they are tied to an account with minimal risk in the event my privacy was to be invaded, such as the *Public Trust Account*.[3] Otherwise, one could arrange to use a cash deposit in lieu of using a debit card.

GIFT CARDS

Retail stores sell gift cards with the Visa and MasterCard logo on the card. Generally, the amounts range from $25 to $100.

The value of these cards is in the ability for the user to make anonymous purchases online or elsewhere. These cards may be registered in any name you choose.

Two gift cards I have used that may be purchased for anonymous use are listed below. Check the websites for a convenient location near you.

Simon Gift Card ($500 limit)
Web: www.simon.com/giftcard

ACE Cash Express ($250 limit)
Web: www.acecashexpress.com

DIGITAL GOLD PAYMENTS

I once looked into using digital gold as a means of making anonymous payments. This is a wonderful system but with some problems occurring from time to time.

My discoveries indicated that some of these accounts had been frozen by "you know who" and that payments received were difficult to convert into cash anonymously. This kept me from using any of these services.

At this time, I do not use these services for paying bills. Please investigate for yourself and keep up with developments in this industry.

BARTER

I expect we have all bartered, without the full realization of doing it, sometime during our lives.

A standardized barter system is not necessary for normal barter transactions. In fact, barter appears to be the ultimate free market system as a means of exchange for needed goods and services, as it provides for the negotiation of values assigned to business goods and services.

ALTERNATVE CURRENCIES

As previously mentioned, NORFED tried to create a responsible, asset-backed currency, only to have their money and assets seized.

Today, a new currency or two has surfaced, advocating some of the same principles as the old NORFED system (see Chapter 1) that was raided and shut down by the FBI. NORFED was an asset-backed system of exchange.

ADDENDUM:

In March, 2011, NORFED founder Bernard von NotHaus was convicted by a federal jury of making, possessing, and selling his own coins.

Von NotHaus faces a 15-year prison sentence and a fine of not more than $250,000.00 for distributing the coins as money. Additionally, he received a second sentence of five years and fines of $250,000.00 related to making the Liberty Dollar coins—and to a conspiracy charge.

CASHLESS SOCIETY

I doubt those who tout the coming "cashless society" have any accurate time targets for such a drastic change to occur in the system. I do not at this time take their claims seriously that a "cashless society" is coming soon.

Cash is a huge part of free trade, and to outlaw its use seems unlikely during the next decade or two.

Use cash as a means of exchange today and in the future, whenever it is practical to do so to enhance your financial privacy.

SUMMARY

1. Major credit bureaus track and trace borrowers' transactions. Users of credit may have their business and personal privacy invaded. Certain borrowers may disguise their borrowing to avoid these privacy invasions. Freezing credit bureau files may limit the number of creditors who have access to personal credit bureau files.

2. Cash and money orders have been used successfully to avoid the tracking of the sources of funds to pay bills. Avoid structuring when paying bills with cash.

3. Cashier's checks, personal and business checks, Automatic Clearing House transactions, and bank wires enable the receiver of the funds and others to trace the origination of the account used to pay the bill.

4. MoneyGram and Western Union provide electronic transfers for paying bills with reasonable privacy. Receivers of funds through these sources will have to provide identification to the agent.

5. Credit cards, gift cards, and debit cards may be appropriate for paying bills with various degrees of anonymity.

NOTES:

1. Grant Hall, *Privacy Crisis: Identity Theft Prevention Plan and Guide to Anonymous Living* (Las Vegas , NV: James Clark King, LLC, 2006), 374; http://www.privacycrisis.com.

2. W. G. Hill, *Banking in Silence* (Plymouth, England: Scope International, Limited, 1998), 201.

3. Hall, Ibid.

Reflections and New Beginnings

I opened my first bank account at age 8 without identification or a Social Security Number. Withdrawals were made with only the passbook as an account identifier, much like the Austrian Sparbuch account transactions, without problems or interference from government watchdogs. Others did the same in America and Europe, as financial privacy was an accepted standard at the time.

I lived and worked during the wonderful era of the 1980s in America, spent time in Europe, and never dreamed the Swiss bankers and others would do anything except continue with their bank secrecy traditions. Nor did I anticipate having to cope with the financial privacy invasions we face today from our government and others.

Changes—even drastic, negative changes—are not without promise, as new pathways emerge into highways of opportunity for those with the foresight to see them. Bright, ambitious businesspeople dream of new opportunities to rev up the creative engines that will drive tomorrow's innovative goods and services. Capitalism is wonderful, when it is allowed to flourish. Freedom is a natural state for the civilized, educated, thinking human being. Will America flourish and be free again?

Sadly, American and other governments are not on the side of freedom seekers or capitalists today but rather have demonstrated their intentions to crush free market systems and free people. Today's system is designed to redistribute wealth unjustly, rather than to foster its creation.

Make no mistake about it: Financial privacy and bank secrecy are undesirable freedoms for the fascists who control masses of the population. Accountability of assets and taxpayers are essential powers to enrich the controllers, as they experiment with unprecedented executive orders and other communist-style policies.

The socioeconomic trend for the U.S. and certain Western European countries is toward a new world order designed to dictate to and take from freedom-seeking, capitalist-minded businesspeople. The middle class is being wiped out, as labor cheapens and entrepreneurship is discouraged by excessive taxes and unreasonable regulations designed to stomp out small businesses, while the bottom lines of monopoly-like conglomerates strengthen.

I reflect from time to time on what could have been a more equal opportunity for many who aspired to enjoy and practice the freedoms promised by our founders. Many of us simply want to exercise our freedoms and be left alone, while employing government to provide minimal, essential services. We don't want what has been forced upon us today. We live in unusual times, with awareness increasing as the American dream becomes a nightmare for too many.

Despite the sub-optimal conditions of the times, it is possible to establish a Privacy Crisis Banking plan. I hope you will make maximum use of the resources and principles I've outlined in this book. Everything you need is here—all you need is the dedication to study, learn, and implement these practices to ensure a brighter tomorrow, with your capital and savings intact.

Index

Bibliography

ARTICLES/ONLINE REFERENCES:

_____. "Child Maintenance Agency Moves to Seize 340 Non-Payers' Homes." *Guardian.co.uk.* February 7, 2010. http://www.guardian.co.uk/society/2010/feb/07/child-maintenance-houses-seized.

_____. "Liechtenstein Eases Bank Secrecy Amid Tax Crackdown." *elEconomista.es.* December 3, 2009. http://www.eleconomista.es/empresas-finanzas/noticias/1094855/03/09/Liechtenstein-eases-bank-secrecy-amid-tax-crackdown.html.

_____. "Swiss Government Bows to Court Ruling: Will Review UBS Tax Agreement." Accounting Web.com. January 28, 2010. http://www.accountingweb.com/topic/tax/swiss-government-bows-court-ruling-will-review-ubs-tax-agreement.

Barlow, John Perry (EFF). "In Decrypting the Puzzle Palace." *Communications of the ACM,* vol. 35, No. 7, July 1992.

Browne, Harry. "Does the Constitution Contain a Right to Privacy?" 2003. www.HarryBrowne.org.

Dunbar, Elizabeth. "Former Wells Fargo Bank Teller Charged with Stealing 100K." Minnesota Public Radio. August 6, 2010. http://minnesota.publicradio.org/display/web/2010/08/06/former-wells-fargo-teller-charged-with-stealing-100k.

Gathright, Alan. "Bank Officer Accused of Stealing $1 Million From Widow." *Denver News.* http://www.thedenverchannel.com/news/21946280/detail.html.

Goodwin, Dan. "IT insider Admits Stealing info for 2,000 Bank Employees: Makes off with 1.1M." *The Register.* July 2, 2010. http://www.theregister.co.uk/2010/07/02/bank_insider_data_theft.

Greenspan, Alan. "Gold and Economic Freedom." 1966. http://www.321gold.com/fed/greenspan/1966.html.

Griffin, R. Morgan. "The Scary Truth about Medical Identity Theft." *WebMD.* February 2, 2007. http://www.webmd.com/a-to-z-guides/features/scary-truth-medical-identity-theft.

Hall, Grant. "Nevada Limited Partnership: Bulletproof Asset Protection." December 20, 2008. http://www.privacycrisis.com/nevada_limited_partnership.html.

Hall, Grant. "The Money Privacy Crisis: 'Banking Secretly in the U.S.A.'" January 5, 2010. http://www.lewrockwell.com/orig10/hall-g2.1.1.html.

Hall, Grant. "Trust Manager Principle: Avoid a Business Privacy Invasion." February, 2009. http://www.privacycrisis.com/trust_manager_principle.html.

Herpel, Mark. "NORFED Dissolved By The Board, 'Liberty Services,' dba, 'Liberty Dollar' Emerges." *American Chronicle.* December 28, 2006. http://Americanchronicle.com/articles/views/18406.

Hornberger, Jacob C. "The Soviet-Style Attack on NORFED," *The Future of Freedom Foundation.* November 21, 2007. http://www.fff.org/comment/com0711j.asp.

Ignatius, Jeff. "The Future of Money? With the Economy in a Wreck, Alternative Currencies Could Gain." *Berkshares, Inc.,* February 4, 2009. www.berkshares.org/press/09feb04.htm.

Jones, Steven E. "Why Indeed Did the WTC Buildings Completely Collapse?" *Journal of 911 Studies.* September, 2006, vol. 3. http://www.journal911studies.com.

Kavanaugh, Kelli B. "3 Cheers for Detroit's Local Currency." April 21, 2009. http://www.modeldmedia.com/features/detroitcheers18809.aspx.

Leamy, Elizabeth. "Not-So-Safe-Deposit Boxes: States Seize Citizens' Property to Balance Their Budgets." ABC News, Good Morning America. May 12, 2008. http://abcnews.go.com/GMA/story?id=4832471&page=1.

MacGillis, Alec. "Federal Raid on Money Group Riles Ron Paul Supporters." *The Seattle Times.* November 17, 2007. http://www.modeldmedia.com/features/detroitcheers18809.aspx.

Nicholson, Kiernan. "Hundreds of Patients at Risk of ID Theft." December 7, 2007. http://www.denverpost.com/ci_7660967?source=bb.

Nimmo, Kurt. "Dollar Devaluation and Destruction of America Pick up Steam." July 11, 2010. http://www.infowars.com/dollar-devaluation-and-destruction-of-america-pick-up-steam.

Powell, Chris. "Mistakenly Disclosed Affidavit Outlines Case Against Liberty Dollar." November 18, 2007. http://news.goldseek.com/GATA/1195420514.php>; <http://www.johnlocke.org/site-docs/meckdeck/pdfs/USAVLibdoll.pdf.

Rogers, Jim (ed.). "Bernanke Doesn't Know What He's Doing."

November 10, 2010. http://wallstreetpit.com/50092-jim-rogers-bernanke-doesnt-know-what-hes-doing.

Rongstad, Jim. "Montana Governor Brian Schweitzer Tells Feds to Go to Hell." March 7, 2008. http://rongstad.blogspot.com/2008/03/montana-governor-brian-schweitzer-tells.html.

Ryter, John Christian. "FBI Raids Liberty Dollar." *News With Views. com.* November 17, 2007. http://newswithviews.com/ryter/jon201.htm.

Shaw, Don. "Liberty Dollar Maker, Three Others Arrested by Feds." *Evansville Courier & Press.* June 5, 2009. http://www.courierpress.com/news/2009/jun/05/05web-LibertyDollar.

Webster, Michael. "Federal Government Closes Down Liberty Dollar," *Bonds Market.* July 16, 2010. http://bondsmarket.org/federal.government-closes-down-liberty-dollar.

White, Ben. "Bernanke Unwrapped." *The Washington Post.* November, 15, 2005. http://www.washingtonpost.com/wp-dyn/content/article/2005/11/14/AR2005111401544.html.

Wolf, Naomi. "Banks Siding Against the Customer in Fraud Cases." *The Huffingon Post.* August 23, 2010. http://www.huffingtonpost.com/naomi-wolf/post_722_b_691188.html.

Wollstein, Jarret. "Police Confiscations Still Out of Control." Novemeber 19, 2008. International Society for Individual Liberty. http://www.isil.org/resources/fnn/2001june/usa-police-confiscations.html.

Woods, R. Glenn. "Effective Strategies for Asset Protections: Gifts, Exemption, Limited Partnership, and Nevada and Offshore Protection Trusts." Woods,, Erickson, Whitaker & Maurice, LLP. 2001–2009. http:www.woodserickson.com/article5.html, http://www.woodserickson.com.

Zash, Chelsi, and Justin Quesberry. "Chatham County Community

Creates Currency." April 6, 2009. http://www.digtriad.com/
news/local_state/article.aspx?storyid=122045.

BLOG POSTS

Rate It All. http://www.rateitall.com/i-18935-etrade.aspx

BOOKS

_____. The Declaration of Independence and the Constitution
of the United States of America. Washington, D.C.: Cato
Institute, 2002.

Barber, Hoyt. *Tax Havens Today.* (Hoboken, NJ: John Wiley &
Sons, Inc., 2006).

Berkman, Gene. *The Trilateral Commission & The New World
Order,* third printing. Riverside, CA: Renaissance
Bookservice, 1992.

Bugliosi, Vincent. *The Prosecution of George W. Bush for Murder.*
New York, NY: Vanguard Press, 2008.

Capote, Truman. *In Cold Blood.* New York, NY: Random House,
New York, 2002.

Corsi, Jerome R., Ph.D. *The Late Great U.S.A.* Los Angeles, CA:
Word Ahead Media, 2007.

Grandpa. *Offshore Banking Secrets Big Brother Doesn't Want You
to Know About.* Saint Vincent and the Grenadines, BWI:
Global Liberty Publishing, Inc., 2009.

Grandpa, et al. *The Invisible Investor: How to Take Your Money
Out of the Country Before Your Country Takes Your Money
Out of You.* Saint Vincent and the Grenadines, BWI: Global
Liberty Publishing, 1997–2009.

Griffin, Edward G. *The Creature From Jekyll Island: A Second Look at the Federal Reserve,* Fourth Edition. Westlake Village, CA: American Media, 2002.

Hall, Grant. *Privacy Crisis: Identity Theft Prevention Plan and Guide to Anonymous Living.* Las Vegas, NV: James Clark King, LLC, 2006.

Hill, W. G. *Banking in Silence.* Plymouth, England: Scope International, Limited, 1998.

Hill, W. G. *PT.* Raffles City, Singapore: Expat World, 1998.

Hill, W. G. *PT 2: The Practice.* Plymouth, England: Scope International, Limited, 1990.

Klein, Naomi. *The Shock Doctrine: The Rise of Disaster Capitalism.* New York, NY: Henry Holt and Company, 2007.

Luna, J. J. *Invisible Money.* Canary Islands, Spain: Canary Islands Press, 2009.

Mullins, Eustace. *Secrets of the Federal Reserve: The London Connection,* first edition. Staunton, VA: Bankers Research Institute, 1983.

Orwell, George. *1984.* New York, NY: Signet Classics, 1950.

Party, Boston T. *One Nation Under Surveillance: Privacy From the Watchful Eye.* Gillette, WY: Javelin Press, 2009.

Quigley, Carroll. *Tragedy and Hope: A History of the World in Our Time.* New York, NY: Macmillan, 1966.

RCN, et al., eds. *Common Sense II: America Betrayed,* third printing. Spirit Lake, ID: The Idaho Observer, 2005.

Rothbard, Murray N. *What Has Government Done to Our Money? and The Case for a 100 Percent Gold Dollar,* fifth edition. Auburn, AL: Ludwig von Mises Institute, 2005.

Wolfe, Claire. *The Freedom Outlaw's Handbook: 179 Things To Do 'Til The Revolution.* Boulder, CO: Paladin Press, 2007.

DOCUMENTS

Supreme Court of the State of New York, County of New York: NAOMI WOLF v. JPMORGAN CHASE & Co., INDEX NO. 651288/2010, August 17, 2010. http://i.cdn. turner.com/dr/teg/tsg/release/sites/default/files/assets/ naomiwolfcomplaint.pdf.

United States District Court, Western District of North Carolina, Asheville Division, North Carolina: Application and Affidavit for Seizure Warrant, Seizure Warrant, Case: 1:07-mj-00119-DLH, November 9, 2007.

United States District Court, Western District of North Carolina, Asheville Division: United States of America v. 3,039.375 Pounds of Copper Coins, et al., Case: 1:08-cv-00230-LHT-DLH, May 29, 2008.

VIDEOS AND RADIO INTERVIEWS

"Alan Grayson: 'Which Foreigners Got the Fed's 500,000,000,000?' Bernanke: 'I Don't Know.'" *YouTube. com.* July 21, 2009. http://www.youtube.com/ watch?v=n0NYBTkE1yQ.

"Man Wrongly Accused of Being a 'Deadbead Dad.'" *VodPod.com.* February 21, 2010. http://vodpod.com/watch/3095884-man-wrongly-accused-of-being-a-deadbeat-dad?u=mgtow&c=mgtow.

"Senator Sanders Goes Off on Bernanke." *YouTube.com.* March 3, 2009. http://www.youtube.com/watch?v=rCWXrMCGJT4.

"Unidentified Reporter questions Bush on camera, Bush Admits That Iraq Had Nothing to Do with 911." *YouTube.com.*

Interview date unknown; posted on Youtube, August 23, 2006. http://www.youtube.com/watch?v=f_A77N5WKWM.

Freeman, Ian, and Mark Edge. Radio Interview, quote by Bernard von NotHause. Free Talk Live. November 17, 2007. http://libertyring.blogspot.com/2007/11/bernard-von-nothaus-on-free-talk-live.html.

Silverstein, Larry (leaseholder, World Trade Center). "America Rebuilds: A Year at Ground Zero." Interview; PBS Documentary. 2002. http://www.youtube.com/watch?v=Y7lSC3jXFDE.